'WHEN YOU SIT AT THE TABLE WITH YOUR BROTHERS,
SIT LONG, FOR IT IS A TIME THAT IS NOT COUNTED
AGAINST YOU AS PART OF YOUR LIVES.'

PROPHET MUHAMMAD

To Amouleh.

In loving memory of my late uncle,
Elias George Daniel,
who jewelled life for all that crossed his path
with love, laughter, food and generosity.

BETHANY KEHDY

THE JEWELLED TABLE

COOKING, EATING & ENTERTAINING
THE MIDDLE EASTERN WAY

PHOTOGRAPHY BY NASSIMA ROTHACKER

hardie grant books

1

BACK TO BASICS

2

OASIS FOUND

REFRESHMENTS, DIGESTIVES
AND COCKTAILS

3

DECORATE THE TABLE

CRUDITÉS, CANAPÉS AND
PRET-A-MANGER

4

UNFASTEN THE APPETITE

SMALL PLATES AND
ADDITIONAL DISHES

125

5

SHARE THE FEAST

LARGE PLATES AND
PRINCIPAL DISHES

185

6

NEVER-ENDING FEAST

DESSERTS

237

A little over four years ago, I went back to the writing board, (this was a year after publishing my debut book, *The Jewelled Kitchen*). I had so much I wanted to say, explore and research. I ended up going off on several tangents, starting a number of different-themed books yet unable to somehow complete at least one in the first two years I had naively dictated to myself as a suitable time frame. Amongst all this, life happened too, of course. This wasn't the book I thought would come next, but now it makes sense that it does.

I've been exploring and writing about Middle Eastern food for 12 years now. I launched my blog in 2008, a time when talking about labneh and za'atar was like talking about Martian ingredients. Before then, I had begun documenting family recipes and kitchen failures in around the autumn of 2003. I acknowledge the longest measure of my never-ending love affair with Middle Eastern food is that I'd survived on this diet since before I could walk, or I suppose talk. My favourite food is without a doubt the cuisine of my heritage (this wasn't the case during a couple of rebellious years), and a week without this food would be a challenge comparable to balancing on a unicycle!

So how did I learn to cook all this food? I did not attend culinary school, nor did I train under acclaimed chefs. Rather, I've learned to cook by watching, smelling, touching and tasting, just like my ancestors have. The logic and science of cooking are not at the forefront of the home-cooked meals I grew up on, but I've learned to adapt to the nature of measuring ingredients so that others could cook my food. Though really, my cooking has mostly been inspired by this *nafas*. In the Middle East, nafas loosely translates to 'soul cooking' and I learned to cook with nafas – my intuition and senses – by watching, improvising and adapting to my circumstances (whether for time, effort, mood, season, terroir, etc.) but also by incessantly savouring the ongoing development of a dish. The triumphs and disappointments are ongoing. I also learned to cook because I've always listened to my body's whispers of unrebukable cravings.

I hope you find inspiration in this book, to cook and express yourself. Everything that I've shared here is to inspire you to cook with an open appetite, with nafas and generosity so that you may adapt to your taste and to what's available to you at all times of the year. After all, this is the Middle Eastern way of cooking. I hope you may also savour the bits of history and culture throughout.

Yalla! Get your mouneh fermenting, decorate the table, unfasten your appetite and share a (never-ending) feast. This is the hospitable life!

Sofra Daimeh,
BETHANY XX

WELCOME TO THE JEWELLED TABLE

The Middle East is a cradle of lavish feasting, epitomised in its jewelled tables. Eating in the Middle East is both a necessity and a social ritual, and while most Middle Eastern cookbooks understandably focus on the mezze ritual of eating or feasting, it's merely one side of the table! To truly gain a more wholesome perspective of the cuisine requires first, an invitation to a home-cooked meal and second, some history on the matters of feasting in the region, hospitality and the mezze table itself (see Mezze mania, page 264).

In the Middle East, there is a basic split between what is served in the home and what is served outside of it. Restaurant food generally includes two categories: leisurely, social eating, in the case of mezze, or grab-and-eat, fast foods (sit down or on-the-go) such as shawarma, kebabs, or the souk's specials.

The nucleus of the culinary repertoire of the Middle East is the home kitchen. While a mezze table (and the street kitchen) shares much of the same dishes, the distinction between mezze and home-style eating in the Middle East lies not in the edible components that make up either meal, per se, but rather, in the manner or style of serving.

At the most basic distinction, mezze is a procession, whereby there is no real main or principal dish, aside from a focus on drinking, arak (*raki*) or wine, while nibbling and socialising at leisure – around a series of small plates that make up the meal. Meanwhile, the anatomy of an everyday, home-style meal, while still sharing much of the same dishes, weaves around a principal dish, namely stews and rice. This tends to remain true even for a Middle Eastern *aazeemeh* (invitation to guests to a home gathering and meal) whereby the central focus of the meal remains around a principal dish though shifts from stews to whole beasts. Rice remains the common denominator.

This book and its chapters are bound in the style one goes about jewelling a table at home in the Middle East – whether for everyday feasts or for celebratory feasts – always much inspired by the season and hospitality.

THE HOSPITABLE DESERT

The spice essential to any Middle Eastern feast? Hospitality! What we call *karam*... The gregarious hospitality of the Middle East is further emboldened by religion and landscape. The harsh, desolate environment of the desert, stretched across vast swathes of the region, made any traveller's journey a tale of circumstance. The communities that settled around the oases were vital shelters for these wanderers and so a desert code of hospitality evolved to protect both the households and the strangers.

The religious tenets of Islam proclaim a guest to be a gift of God; likewise, the Old Testament of the Bible commands us to protect guests, who might be angels in disguise. And so, under the desert code, the host was obliged to provide food, water and shelter for any traveller who stopped at their tents; turning them away was considered an act of hostility comparable with murder. Guests were greeted with tea or water (one of the many traditions that have transcended the centuries) and often a servant would wash their feet. To refuse such hospitality would also be considered an insult and a hostile reaction. Within these customs, the host would expect protection from any enmity on behalf of the 'stranger' and thus these customs protected both the host and guests.

These notions seep into the art of eating and entertaining in the region and, even today, good manners dictate that a guest is served tea or coffee on arrival, and such an offer must never be rejected.

Which is why a Middle Eastern host is always ready to welcome guests and unannounced visitors; the table is always large and jewelled enough for extra diners. In turn, a guest should always expect to be urged towards several helpings, and the more the guest eats the more appeased the host. The feast seems to never cease. And so for thousands of years, food and hospitality have been thickly woven into a culture bursting with tradition; at its axis, the family or tribe.

THROW THEM A FEAST

The key to any jewelled table is to provide an array of condiments and sides, always a salad and more often than not a platter of rice. Soups are also popular and may be served to start the meal, especially in the instance of breaking a fast. Bread, a staple, is indispensable to the Middle Eastern culinary experience, often replacing utensils.

A basic home meal will include a grain and vegetarian or meat stew, pickles, salad and yoghurt. Also on the table are bread, olives, pickles and/or raw vegetables. A more formal, home-style meal for company will include appetisers (*muqabilat*) followed by two main dishes (usually a stew, stuffed vegetables or meat) and salad. The muqabilat remain on the table throughout the meal, along with the bread, olives, pickles and raw vegetables all part of the table's decoration. Once dessert is served – which is typically coffee, fruit or pastry – only then are the main dishes cleared away. Often, the dessert and coffee are served in a separate room, such as the salon.

WHAT'S MINE IS OURS

Cultural assimilation, appropriation, diffusion, fusion and cross-fusion of cuisine (and culture!) has been constant since the dawn of civilisation. History tells us that cuisine has always been adaptive and adoptive by virtue of trade but also kneaded, shaped and slow-baked by empires – their expansion, invasions as well as migration and diasporas.

While it may appear like the food of the Middle East has remained relatively unchanged since the dawn of time due to the tendency of strict observation of tradition in the Middle East, it is in fact a cuisine that has been privy to a fair share of change. A brief example is the adoption of non-native ingredients, such as the aubergine (see Lady Buran, page 145) and the tomato into Middle Eastern cuisine (see Maftoul-stuffed turnips, page 210). We know the ancient Greeks refined their cooking by learning from the ancient Persians, in turn offering up inspiration to the ancient Romans with plenty of cross-fusion as well. The Mongols fused Persian and Chinese culinary culture and, later, cooks of Medieval Europe were greatly influenced by the food of the Arab world.

SO WHAT IS THE FOOD OF THE ARAB WORLD?

Many of the dishes we may arbitrarily call Lebanese, Palestinian or Syrian are dishes that are, in fact, shared across the national boundaries of what has been historically referred to as the Levant or Mashriq or *bilad el sham* or 'countries of the North', which encompassed modern-day Syria, Lebanon, Palestine and Israel, Jordan and southern parts of Turkey.

That's because today's geographical boundaries are century-old borders drawn by the colonial powers of the era. For most of the aforementioned nations, there is no distinct national cuisine per se; instead, micro-distinctions and nuances exist, which may be influenced by rural life, terroir and micro-localised ingredients or traditions. Lines of culinary tradition can therefore resemble a sauce-smeared plate, though there does exist distinguishing national dishes that may or may not be shared, and that come to the forefront in specific countries. Examples of this are the Musakkhan of Palestine, a dish celebrating the olive oil harvest and the desert rice, meat and dry yoghurt dish (see Jameed, page 100), known as Mansaf and particular to Jordan, though the theme is ubiquitous across the Arabian Gulf.

For the most part though, these countries' cuisine reflects their shared ancestry, tradition (though not necessarily religion), language, and the empires that passed through their kitchens. Therefore, it's not a novelty to see a dozen adaptations and namesakes for the same dish. Of course, there are lesser known traditions and distinct dishes to each country which have not made their way into the proliferation of today's cookbooks, whether Arabic or foreign language. The food of most of the population – that is of poor or rural people – was snubbed and rarely chewed by the noblemen and so would remain relatively obscure, never staining a manuscript. This is again because empires, not city-states, have influenced and forged cuisines.

Yet even with so many obvious similarities, the cuisine of the greater region does not remain so uniform with further idiosyncrasies and nuances but also more striking divisions. This is true with the food of the Persian or Arabian Gulf and North Africa. To more accurately examine (though not absolutely) Middle Eastern food is to then slice the cake in three; Levantine cuisine, Persian or Arabian gulf cuisine and North African cuisine. At its root is the oldest cuisine in the world, the dusty Mesopotamian kitchen of modern-day Iraq and parts of Iran, Syria and Turkey. Finally, one must then also mingle with the empires that have permeated the banquets of the region; the Ottomans, the Abbasid Caliphate, the Mogols and the Persian Empire to really savour the full-bodied history and uniqueness of Middle Eastern food.

THE ISRAELI FRONT

Today, Israeli food is the front-runner of Middle Eastern cuisine – much like Greek food was in the 90s and 2000s – an example is how the West associated hummus with the Greeks, even though the dish isn't part of the Greek culinary repertoire. Ask for hummus in Greece a decade ago and you'd have been met with puzzled looks. Yet, in the West hummus was heavily marketed as Greek!

Today we see the same thing happen, humorously one of the casualties is hummus again, though 'Israeli' is the darling marketing word. Hummus, while the *habibi* of the whole levant, is in fact believed (to date) to be of Egyptian origin. What I wish to say though, is Israeli food should by no means be a benchmark or a footprint of Levantine or Middle Eastern cuisine as a whole – a cuisine historically shared by Muslims, Christians and Jews inhabiting the region – as the trend likes to serve up. A recently established country and largely made up by colonialists, the food of Israel is a melting-pot of the adopted Levantine and Arab cuisine (as they also refer to it within Israel) as well as the cultures of the near and far countries the colonisers came from during the last century. Which is why, the food and culture of Israel is in no way an authentic reflection of Middle

Eastern or Levantine cuisine but rather a fusion of Jewish diaspora cuisine and indigenous cuisine.

To save the debate of cultural appropriation versus cultural appreciation for another platform, as politics cannot but spill hot oil in the kitchen, I will finish by saying Israel is of course allowed its own national cuisine as it is also allowed to decide what will be its national dish, even if that dish is one adopted from the Arabic kitchen. After all, as history has shown us about the influences highlighted in much of this book, our kitchen is very much the drumming result of banging pots and pans and the cross-fusion between our kitchens and those of the empires that have conquered us. Cuisine cannot be confined and cuisine should not be confined! Rather than break dishes, we need to be breaking bread. However, we must be as translucent as a perfectly sweated onion, Israeli cuisine is not Levantine or Middle Eastern cuisine, it's a fusion-cuisine and much inspired by the indigenous food of the terroir it has colonised. One need only allow the Arabic, Turkish or Persian (generally speaking) etymology of the dishes speak for themselves.

PANTRY ESSENTIALS

To build a satiating feast, one must begin with a well-stocked pantry; be flexible and adapt with the season's bounty and understand the basics of Middle Eastern cooking and seasoning. All of these ingredients can be found online if they cannot be sourced at your local supermarket.

Aleppo pepper closely resembling the Ancho pepper in flavour, hails from Aleppo, Syria, but are also grown in neighbouring Turkey and known as Isot Biber. They are a bright red, mildly spicy pepper, with a high oil content and a hint of fruity sweetness with earthy, smoky tones.

Argan oil is a nutty-tasting oil that comes from the fruit of the argan tree, which grows in south-western Morocco. It has been used by the Berber people for centuries for its medicinal properties as well as in cooking (especially in tagines and couscous). It can also be mixed with honey and eaten with bread or pancakes.

Barberries are beautiful, red, jewel-like dried fruits that are bursting with tartness. If you cannot find them, subsitite with cranberries.

Burghul, also known as bulgur, is a very nutritious, highly-versatile grain. It is a wheat grain that has been boiled, sun-dried, hulled and ground to varying grades, which means it is technically a preserved wheat! This processing allows it to resist infestation by pests. It's believed burghul is produced using an ancient process that originated in Mesopotamia, the region of modern-day Kurdistan, though there is no real proof of its origin or mention before the 13th century. From an etymological standpoint, the likeliest candidate for the origin of the word may be the Kurdish *palkhurd* meaning 'crushed' or 'small pebbles' though modern-day kurds now call it Savar. In Arabic, it is called 'burghul' (via Persian bulgur), and has the same meaning. However, modern-day Iranians rarely ever use the grain. So, when and by who burghul came to be is elusive (with claims of it mentioned in the Bible), but the general consensus is that the (Ottoman) Turks were the ones who helped spill the grain across their empire. Burghul is a whole grain. Lighter colours indicate where the bran has been removed, which is why it's best to opt for the more wholesome reddish-brown varieties. The burghul you find in Western supermarkets is limited to medium grain. However, there exists a distinction based on how it is used in dishes. In Turkey, the finer grades are called *köftelik bulgur*, used in the kofte- and kebbeh-themed dishes, a burghul salad called *kisir*, and tabbouleh, while the coarser varieties are called *pilavlik bulgur* and used in pilafs, soups and stews. An identification ranging from fine (#1), medium (#2 & #3) and coarse (#4) also exists.

Carob molasses is a dark caramel natural sweetener made by cooking the carob pod with water, then straining and reducing it down to a thick syrup. It was the traditional sweetener alongside honey.

Dried limes are green limes which have been dried in the sun until they become very hard. They can range from sandy-white or black, depending on how long they have been left to dry – the darker limes have a stronger, more musky and fermented note. They are used to lend a unique sharp, astringent flavour to fish stews and dishes rich in pulses and meats. They may be punctured, broken open and the seeds removed or ground to a powder before being used.

Freekeh is an ancient grain and cereal made from green wheat, which is native to many parts of the Middle East and North Africa. It has a nutty undertone and a smoky aroma. It is high in fibre, protein, vitamins and minerals and may be suitable for gluten-free diets (please consult your doctor) as the gluten is denatured due to the high-temperature burning process. It can be purchased cracked and whole, and might require careful cleaning to rid it of any stones.

Grape molasses is one of the oldest sweeteners, made by reducing fresh grapes down into a caramel-coloured syrup. It is packed with a host of health benefits.

Maftoul is an earthy, Palestinian 'pasta' similar to couscous, though its rolled from wheat and differs in size, colour and shape. These grains cook unevenly because they are rolled into inconsistently sized balls. They swell and become soft and chewy when cooked and are fantastic at absorbing the flavours of the dish they are cooked in. If you're unable to find maftoul, use fregola.

Mahlab is a spice derived from the sour cherry stones of the St Lucia tree (*Prunus mahaleb*). The kernels from these crimson-red cherries are ground to an aromatic powder. The flavour is a combination of bitter almond and cherry. Mahlab, ground or whole, is used to flavour dishes around the Middle East. If the recipe calls for actual sour cherries use morello cherries.

Mastic is a gum and an aromatic resin that is cultivated from the bark of the Mediterranean mastic tree. It is crushed and used in powder form in many desserts in parts of the Mediterranean and across the Middle East. Use mastic tears (drop-shaped pieces of the resin) or powder sparingly because the flavour can be overpowering.

Mulberry syrup is a reduction of mulberries and sugar to a thick syrup. It is used traditionally to make *sharabs*, or soft drinks.

Salep flour is milled from the dried tubers of a wild orchid species found in the Anatolian plateau. It is used in a popular milk and spice beverage of the same name and also a light and stretchy ice cream. Salep can be quite hard to find and rather expensive, but you could substitute it with cornflour or even some ground mastic.

Shankleesh is a mould-ripened cheese popular to the Levant. It comes formed into balls, like hard labneh, and heavily seasoned with dried za'atar, cumin, hot pepper and nigella seeds. It is typical to the mezze table.

Sumac is a tangy, deep red or burgundy spice derived from the dried berries of the sumac bush. It is used along with lemon or in place of lemon to add a tart, citrusy flavour to dishes as well as meats, fried eggs and dips.

Tahini from the Arabic root word *tahan* or 'to grind' is pronounced theené or theena, depending on one's dialect. Tahini is a tan-coloured paste made from raw or lightly-roasted sesame seeds. A good quality tahini is the result of high-quality sesame seeds; and the best and whitest of sesame seeds are said to come from Humera in Ethiopia. The processing is as important. The best tahini is single-origin and cold-pressed, where the temperature does not exceed 15°C (60°F) and using traditional grindstones. It's also important that tahini is not adulterated with oils or limestone, which are often used as a whitening agent – separation or hard clumps at the bottom is a red flag. I have always – at all costs – steered away from the supermarket brands; the texture is grainy and the flavour bitter. In particular, I recommend Lebanese or Palestinian brands, but there also seems to be artisanal brands sprouting up. Look for a tahini that has a nutty, light-coloured, silky texture. The main market brands I'd recommend as a starting point are: 365 Organic, Al Taj or Karawan. According to *The Gaza Kitchen* author Laila El-Haddad, there exists a 'rusty-tan' variety called 'red tahini' which is specific to Gaza and is a result of slow-roasting the sesame seeds. However, there is a little confusion on the front of black tahini. The black tahini, sold in most health food stores in the West, is derived from ground black sesame seeds. This is not the same as the Palestinian black paste, called *qizha*, which is made from nigella seeds, locally referred to as 'habt el barakah'.

Verjuice is the unfermented sour juice extracted from semi-ripe grapes. It adds a wonderfully delicate, sweet-tangy tone to dishes, salads and reductions.

I

BACK TO BASICS

CHARRED VEGETABLES

prep   5 minutes
       per vegetable
cook   15–20 minutes
       per vegetable

This is a basic method for chargrilling or roasting vegetables such as aubergines (eggplants), (bell) peppers or tomatoes. They can be prepped up to two days in advance of eating and used in recipes such as the Sfiha stars (page 110) and the Smoked fish kebbeh smørrebrød (page 220). Popping the vegetables straight on the gas hob can be a bit of a mess but the resulting flavours are worth it.

Line the base of a gas hob with foil, leaving the gas burners exposed. Turn the gas hob to a high heat and place the aubergine and/or pepper, stem still on, directly over the burner, turning each one occasionally with tongs until the aubergine or pepper is blackened and charred, and the flesh is soft. This should take about 5 minutes per side or 15–20 minutes in total.

Alternatively, grill using a barbecue or preheat the oven to 200°C/400°F/ Gas 6. Score the aubergine or pepper in a few places to avoid them bursting and cook until all the sides are charred and the flesh is soft.

Remove from the heat and transfer to a resealable plastic bag. Seal the bag and leave to rest for 10 minutes. Holding the stem of the aubergine or pepper one at a time, use the bag to peel off the skin and any charred edges. Discard the skins and strain the flesh of any juices.

TEMPURA ONIONS

makes 227 g (8 oz/
about 2–3 cups)
prep 25 minutes
cook 20 minutes

2 large onions, thinly sliced
1 tablespoon flaky sea salt
4–5 tablespoons plain
(all-purpose) flour
150–250 ml (5 fl oz–8½ fl oz/
1 cup) rapeseed oil

You can make these onions a day in advance of using and store them somewhere dry. I usually put them in the oven, uncovered, overnight (the safest place, especially from humans who will pick the plate clean!). Great served with Aubergine mutabal (page 157) and the Warm salad of greens (page 140).

Place the onions in a colander, sprinkle with the salt and massage the onions to help release the moisture. Leave for about 20 minutes or up to an hour for the onions to soften. Massage a couple of times during this time if you can, but this is not completely necessary.

Set a large frying pan over medium heat, pour in enough oil to come 3 cm (1½ in) up the side of the pan and leave to heat for a couple of minutes.

Squeeze the onions very well to rid them of any more moisture. Tip them onto paper towels and pat dry. Add the flour to a bowl and toss in the onions, making sure to coat them evenly. Add more flour if needed.

Fry the floured onions for 3–4 minutes, in batches, in the hot oil until golden. Use tongs to toss them around a few times in the oil to ensure even colouring. Use a slotted spoon to transfer the onions to a plate lined with paper towels and leave them to cool slightly.

STRAINING YOGHURT FOR LABNEH

makes   325 g (11½ oz) soft
         labneh, 250 g (9 oz)
         firm labneh or
         8 x 30 g (1 oz)
         labneh balls
prep   10 minutes

500 g (1 lb 2 oz) goat's (or
   cow's) milk yoghurt
½ teaspoon flaky sea salt
olive oil

Labneh, or Greek yoghurt, is not interchangeable with regular yoghurt and comes in two consistencies: the thick, yet spreadable kind known simply as labneh or the drier, firmer kind (traditionally made from goat's milk and rolled into balls), known as *labneh malboudeh* (see Labneh three ways, page 97). For the soft spread, the yoghurt usually only needs about 24–48 hours to strain into labneh. Marketing terms for yoghurt on the shelves today include labels such as 'Greek' yoghurt or 'Greek-style' yoghurt, both labels that imply the yoghurt has been strained, which if you skim-the-surface should reflect a soft, spreadable labneh! However, things are not that straightforward. Greek-style yoghurt will have been thickened by some means other than straining, such as thickening agents and emulsifiers, and this can greatly affect the consistency (it's inconsistent) and in turn the end results when cooked with. The most authentic and readily available store-bought option, comparable to a soft, spreadable labneh is the FAGE® brand, which is what I recommend using. If you are using this brand or any other strained-yoghurt of the same consistency, then straining it for spreadable labneh is not necessary as it is already thick enough! However, if you are after a firmer, drier labneh crumb, to make labneh balls, for example, then starting off with the FAGE® brand or one of similar texture, straining for 2 days rather than 3 days should suffice. You may use runny Greek yoghurts and strain them to soft labneh, though I don't think it will save a substantial amount of time in comparison to using simple yoghurt.

To make labneh, you can use sheep, goat, camel, buffalo or yak's yoghurt; each lends a slightly different flavour profile (goat's yoghurt yields the most texture in my opinion). Either way, always start with full-fat yoghurt. If you're up for it, try suspending the bag from your kitchen tap. This is the way we do it in the Middle East, and the best way to develop the flavour. Make sure the tap (and surroundings) is clean and be sure to set aside the labneh bag if you need to use the faucet. The whey from straining the labneh is useful added to stews, ice cream and to make bread. Labneh, both the firm and soft kind, is wonderful served as an appetiser with fresh vegetables such as sliced cucumbers and tomatoes, and/or olives, fresh za'atar or za'atar blend (page 84), olive oil and Mini Arabic bread puffs (page 30).

Combine the yoghurt and salt in a mixing bowl. Line a colander with muslin (cheesecloth) and set over a bowl. Add the yoghurt mixture, gather the muslin and twist tightly. Tie with kitchen string. Transfer the bowl with the colander and muslin bag to the fridge to sit overnight or for up to 24-48 hours for soft labneh.

After straining, you will notice that the whey has separated from the yoghurt into the bowl. The strained yoghurt will be thicker – similar to cream cheese in consistency. If you'd like it thicker and firmer still (and to use in the recipes on pages 84, 97-98 and 112), leave it to strain for 1-2 more days.

To serve, transfer the soft labneh to a serving dish and use a spoon to create a well in the middle. Drizzle with olive oil.

THE YOGHURT CHRONICLES

Yoghurt – the real stuff not artificially flavoured, coloured and thickened simulacrum, burdened with sugar and stripped of its healthy fats among many other things – is believed to be the serendipitous discovery of ancient nomadic pastoralists. Without the advent of refrigeration, especially in a hot climate, milk spoiled quickly, and so for millennia, turning it into yoghurt was the only safe way of consuming it. At that time, herdsmen in Central Asia carried milk in bags made of intestinal gut, which is probably how they discovered that contact with intestinal juices caused the milk to curdle and sour, allowing its conservation for extended periods of time.

The curdled milk of the Mongols is very different to the yoghurt that proliferates in the aisles of Western supermarkets today. In fact, the majority of the commercial yoghurts remain quite removed in flavour, texture and versatility from their inspired roots. It was the Turks who, having adopted yoghurt from Persia, expanded its repertoire and put it to the most varied culinary uses. Traditional yoghurt made from goat's and sheep's milk remains a staple of Middle Eastern countries. It's featured in many guises... it's processed into butter, strained to make soft labneh (aka 'Greek yoghurt'), or further strained and rolled into balls (page 97) or fermented with grains for porridge (pages 102 and 191). It's a drink, and a base for sauces, marinades, and desserts. It can also appear unadulterated as a fixture to every meal. My grandfather had a bowl with everything he ate and lived to an impressive age of 96, which the family attributes to the yoghurt.

AGED BUTTER

Samneh is the clarified butter (or ghee) of the Middle East, though depending on the country it can be found in many guises, seasoned, fermented, aged and, as in this recipe, smoked. The North African version is the boldest and has the strongest flavour. The hot climate sees it buried underground to help prolong its preservation. Like ghee, the butter is cooked to reduce the milk solids and moisture making it a great choice of cooking fat with a high smoking point. I have taken inspiration here from the Ethiopian *niter kibbeh* as I prefer a seasoned fat on hand that helps season my dishes as a bonus.

Samneh has been a popular cooking fat since Sumerian times, but in the 1980s the medical consensus was that vegetable oils and margarine were healthier, and samneh and even olive oil use decreased. Dietary advice has now reversed. Either way, I take the position that if it worked for my ancestors for thousands of years it will work for me.

makes 1 x 200 ml (7 fl oz) jar
prep 10 minutes
cook 20–25 minutes

seeds from 2 cardamom pods
½ teaspoon fenugreek seeds
½ teaspoon cumin seeds
½ teaspoon fennel seeds
450 g (1 lb) unsalted butter
5 garlic cloves, unpeeled
½ small onion, very finely chopped
2.5 cm (1 in) piece ginger, sliced, or ½ tablespoon ground ginger
½ tablespoon ground turmeric
½ teaspoon ground cinnamon
2 cloves
pinch of grated nutmeg
1 tablespoon smoked salt
zest of 1 lemon

In a mortar and pestle, roughly pound the cardamom, fenugreek, cumin and fennel seeds. Add to a saucepan and toss for a minute over low heat. Add the butter and melt. Toss in the remaining ingredients, except the salt and lemon zest, and simmer for about 20 minutes or until the butter separates into a golden liquid and a milky sediment. Spoon out any milk solids, discarding the spices, and strain the liquid through a piece of muslin (cheesecloth) into a sterilised jar. Season with the salt and lemon zest, and stir to dissolve. Cover and leave until the butter cools and solidifies, then seal tightly and transfer to the fridge where it will keep for 6 months. Alternatively, leave at room temperature somewhere cool and dry for 1 week to develop further in flavour, making it more pungent.

Also try: For a milder Levantine version, omit all the spices and add 2 tablespoons of dried and ground za'atar leaves.

MOUKASSARAT MHAMARA

TOASTED NUTS

prep 2 minutes
cook 2–3 minutes

1 tablespoon butter or Aged butter (above)
handful nuts of choice

I prefer to toast nuts in butter rather than dry toasting in the oven, as it lends a more even golden hue, while also complementing the nut's natural oils.

Melt the butter in a small saucepan over low medium heat, and, when the butter foams, add in the nuts. Stir and cook for 2–3 minutes until lightly browned. Using a slotted spoon, transfer to a plate lined with paper towels. These will keep for 2–3 days in an airtight container.

makes   4½ tablespoons
prep   2 minutes
cook   2–3 minutes

1 tablespoon black
   peppercorns
1 teaspoon cumin seeds
1 tablespoon coriander seeds
5 cloves
3 cardamom pods
2–3 small dried red chillies
1 cinnamon stick
½ teaspoon ground nutmeg
½ tablespoon ground ginger
½ tablespoon ground
   turmeric

BEZAR

BEZAR SPICE MIX

Both this tumeric-based spice mix and the Hawayej mix below are cousins of Indian masala. The similarity is likely due to the fact both India and the Gulf fell on the ancient trade routes.

Place a small pan over medium heat, add the black peppercorns, cumin and coriander seeds, cloves, cardamom pods, chillies and cinnamon, and lightly toast, shaking the pan often, for 2–3 minutes, until aromatic.

Transfer to a spice grinder and blitz to a fine powder (or use a mortar and pestle and grind). Stir in the nutmeg, ginger and turmeric then transfer to a jar. Seal well. Store in an airtight jar for up to 3 months in a cool, dark place.

---

makes   2 tablespoons
prep   2 minutes

1 teaspoon ground cloves
1 teaspoon ground allspice
1 teaspoon ground fenugreek
1 teaspoon grated nutmeg
1 teaspoon ground ginger
1 teaspoon ground cinnamon
1 teaspoon freshly ground
   black pepper

SABEH BAHARAT

SEVEN SPICES

This is a popular spice mixture in Lebanon. It works wonderfully as a rub on lamb and beef. *Baharat* simply means 'spices' in Arabic and is not indicative of a specific spice or spice mix.

Mix all the ingredients together and use according to the recipe. Store in an airtight jar in a cool, dark place for up to 3 months.

---

makes   4¾ tablespoons
prep   5 minutes
cook   5 minutes

¼ teaspoon cumin seeds
½ teaspoon fennel seeds
½ teaspoon caraway seeds
3 cardamom pods
½ teaspoon black
   peppercorns
½ teaspoon coriander seeds
2 cloves
1 tablespoon ground
   turmeric
½ teaspoon ground ginger
½ teaspoon ground
   cinnamon

HAWAYEJ

HAWAYEJ SPICE MIX

Hawayej spice mix forms the base of many dishes in Yemeni cuisine. The word *hawayej* translates loosely as 'necessities'. The types of spices and the proportions vary from region to region, as does what you use it in, a stew or a coffee (page 52), for instance. The recipe came to me from my Yemeni friend, Shaima. I've since tinkered with it a little and use it a lot in my cooking (pages 52, 72 and 232).

Toast the first seven spices in a pan over low heat for 2 minutes, until aromatic. Transfer to a spice grinder and blitz to a fine powder (or use a mortar and pestle and grind). Stir in the turmeric, ginger and cinnamon. Store in an airtight jar in a cool, dark place for up to 3 months.

KHOBZ
MINI ARABIC BREAD PUFFS

makes   40–45 puffs,
        6 cm (2½ in)
        in diameter
prep   25 minutes plus
        1 hour for rising
cook   5 minutes

300 g (10½ oz/2 cups)
strong white flour, plus extra
   for dusting
½ teaspoon flaky sea salt
1 teaspoon caster (superfine)
   sugar
60 ml (2 fl oz/¼ cup) olive
   oil
1 teaspoon dried active yeast

No table is correctly decorated without bread, especially so in the Middle East where it's the unequivocal vehicle for consuming foods, used interchangeably with utensils to dip and scoop.

This is a basic recipe for Arabic bread. The shaping can be altered as you wish (see variation, opposite) and the baking time adjusted.

Sift the flour into a mixing bowl, add the sugar and salt, and pour in the oil. Mix well with your hands.

Add the yeast to 150 ml (5 fl oz/scant ⅔ cup) lukewarm water and stir until dissolved. Pour the water and yeast mixture into the flour and oil mixture, little by little, combining with your hands as you go, until a ball forms. You may find that you need more or less water.

Transfer the dough to a well-floured work surface and continue kneading until smooth and elastic. Return the dough to the mixing bowl, then score the top with a knife to loosen the surface tension. Cover with a damp, clean tea towel and place in a warm, draught-free place for about 1 hour or until doubled in size.

Once the dough has doubled in size, turn it out onto a lightly floured work surface and knock it back, then knead gently before rolling it into a log. Cover with a tea towel and set aside.

Preheat the oven to 230°C/450°F/Gas 8 and place a large baking sheet in the oven to warm up.

Divide the log into four balls of equal size, each weighing about 125 g (4 oz). Lightly flour the work surface and use a rolling pin to roll out each ball to 5 mm (¼ in) thick circles, and using a 6 cm (2½ in) pastry cutter, stamp about 12 circles, flouring the surface as necessary. Repeat with the remaining dough balls and scraps. You should end up with roughly 40–48 rounds.

Place the rounds on the warmed baking sheet, spacing them apart to avoid overcrowding. Lightly sprinkle the surfaces of the rounds with water and bake for about 5 minutes, or until the top and edges are lightly golden and a pocket of air has formed. Do not cook them for longer than 1 minute after the air pocket has formed, otherwise they will be brittle. Repeat with the remaining dough rounds.

Remove the breads from the oven and serve immediately. If you're making the breads in advance, cover them with a damp tea towel and allow to cool, then store in a resealable plastic bag. The breads can be kept, wrapped, in a fridge for up to 2–3 days or in the freezer for up to 1–2 months. Allow 20–30 minutes defrosting time before microwaving briefly or baking in a hot oven for 2–3 minutes to heat through.

Also try: Indent the rounds with your fingers to form a bowl shape and brush with a little Za'atar blend (page 84) mixed with olive oil and bake. As for toppings, use any of the kishk or labneh on pages 97–105, or the pizzettes (page 112).

GRIDDLED FLATBREAD VARIATION

makes 4–6
cook 5 minutes

1 x quantity Arabic bread
   (opposite)
flour, for dusting

Make the recipe for the Arabic bread up to the shaping step. Divide the log into four balls of equal size, each weighing about 125 g (4 oz). Lightly flour the work surface and use a rolling pin to roll out each ball into a circle about 20 cm (8 in) in diameter. Alternatively, make larger ones by rolling them out to 30 cm (12 in) rounds. Note that the thinner the dough is rolled the crisper they will be when baked. Bake thinner breads for a shorter time. Cover the loaves with a tea towel and leave to rest 10 minutes.

Place a heavy-based griddle pan over high heat until smoking hot. Sprinkle the surfaces of the rounds with a little water. Place the dough rounds into the pan, without overcrowding, and cook for 1–2 minutes on each side. Remove and serve immediately.

Also try: Arabs will usually toast whole flatbreads directly on gas burners to warm or crisp them up (60 seconds, turning them over once).

KHOBZ MHAMMAS

AYSH PITA PYRAMIDS

serves about 8
prep 5 minutes
cook 1–2 minutes

3–4 small Lebanese
   flatbreads
1–2 tablespoons olive oil
flaky sea salt
ground sumac and/or Za'atar
   blend (page 84) (optional)

I dislike using the word 'pita', since it's reminiscent of thick, chewy, unpliable supermarket breads... but it adds alliteration! Make sure you're using the thin, Lebanese-style flatbread, which you can buy in various diameters. Lavoush or naan bread will work, too. These are great to have as crisp bites to be dipped into za'atar and olive oil, labneh or crumbled to add texture to salads.

Preheat the grill (broiler) to high. Use a knife to slice through the centres of the flatbreads, then use kitchen shears to cut across diagonally, each time in an opposing manner to yield pyramid-like shapes. Arrange on the tray under the grill, and drizzle with the oil and a sprinkle of sea salt. If using, sprinkle with the sumac and/or za'atar. Grill for 1–2 minutes, or until they are golden and crisp. Serve with dip of choice. Keeps well in an airtight container for up to a week.

ARAB BREAD SCOOP

The most common way to eat Arabic bread is by using a method referred to here as the scoop but known colloquially as *teghmees*. This edible spoon can be used to scoop up anything you're eating from your jewelled table. Here is how to master it:

1   Hold a single mini bread puff between your thumb and index finger.

2   Fold the top of the bread puff over the top of your thumb.

3   Fold both sides of the bread puff towards the middle, over the top fold.

4   Remove the scoop from your finger.

5   Use the edible spoon to scoop up all of your delicious dishes.

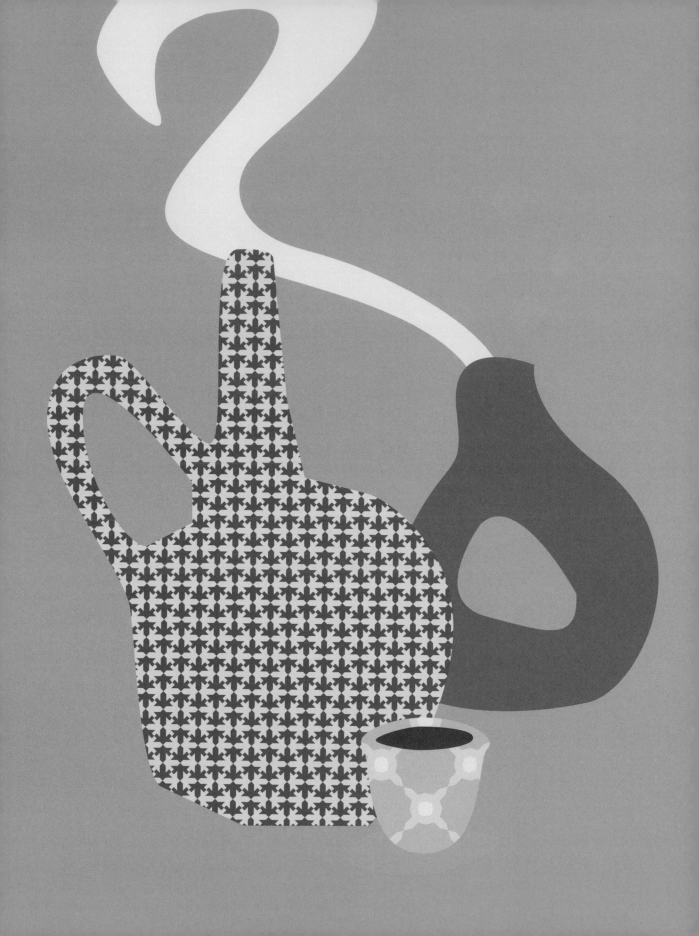

2

OASIS FOUND

**REFRESHMENTS, DIGESTIVES
AND COCKTAILS**

THE WELCOME

A welcome in the Middle East is something almost overwhelming. Guests are of paramount importance, and while the elaborateness with which they are received or welcomed (*al tarheeb*) varies according to the means of the host, one thing is constant and that is the host's effort to make guests feel both comfortable and that they have honoured the house with their presence. Conduct and etiquette in occasions of hospitality are taken seriously, from the details of seating to the order of precedence in serving, and in the manners expected between and of guest and host. Ahead is a summary of the ritual and dance of hospitality.

THE WELCOME: SHARAFTOUNA

The host gives the guest a big bellowing welcome.

Three kisses (minimum), a hand shake, a hug if intimate. Women of strict Islamic guidance do not kiss or shake hands with men outside of their family.

THE GUEST

Comes with hands bearing gifts or homemade delicacies for the host.

AHLAN WA SAHLAN

'YOU HAVE DESCENDED ON YOUR OWN PEOPLE AND YOUR PRESENCE FEELS AS EASY AS ONE HAVING STEPPED UPON THE FLAT PLAINS'

The gist: 'You are an easy guest to welcome, please feel at home'.

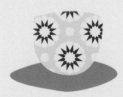

THE HOST

Prepares water, coffee, *shai*, *mashroob*.

On arrival it is imperative that the guest is greeted with coffee, shai, water, and/or *sharab* (fruit juices), tea or coffee (and water) without question. When the guest arrives, the table is already decorated with most of the dishes and the guest may be seated at the table. However, they may also be seated in the *salon* or traditionally the *diwan* to first enjoy coffee or drinks.

THE JEWELLED TABLE

The guest of honour is always offered the best seat in the house, usually the one furthest from the door or *fi al-sadr*, meaning 'at the top of the room' or he may be seated to the right of the host. At the table, the guest is naturally served first and offered the best of the food, the host being extra attentive, making sure the guest's plate is repleted often!

THE DANCE OF HOSPITALITY

The essence of hospitality lies in the amount and variety of food put before a guest and how well one succeeds in feeding it to him or her.

JUST SAY YES

In accepting food, the guest is reserved. A guest will often refuse the food offered to him/her several times (even if they do want it) before they finally accept it. This gives the host a chance to press the food upon the guest, in turn showing their generosity.

GRATITUDE

The guest wishes the host gratitude by saying '*saleem dayetek*' (thanks to your hands) and '*sofra daimeh enshallah*' or 'may this table always be repeated, God willing'.

DRINKS

Alongside tea and coffee – essentials in the Middle Eastern home – there is an eclectic variety of beverages on offer. You'll find hot or cold scented waters, fermented grain drinks, pickled juice, diluted savoury yoghurt (*ayran*), fresh or concentrated syrup-based juices and alcoholic beverages such as the spirit arak and locally bottled beers and wines. The following is in no way comprehensive but will hopefully inspire you to try something new.

MAI

LOADED AQUA – THREE WAYS

Traditionally, distilled essence waters (in particular orange blossom water) would be offered to guests as a sort of cologne – or *kolonya* – to refresh and wash germs off the hands. And much like how the original eau du Cologne was once drunk to repel fleas and ward off plague, one can enjoy these delicious waters and literally exude the essence of the Mediterranean.

WATERMELON, ROSE & MINT AQUA

makes 1.8 litres (61 fl oz)
prep   5 minutes,
          plus chilling time

100 g (3½ oz) watermelon,
  chopped
handful mint leaves,
  roughly chopped
1–2 tablespoons rose water
ice cubes (optional)

Depending on seasons, I'll use any manner of fruit for this. The rose and mint complement mulberries, pomegranates or rhubarb equally. If using rhubarb, soak chopped rhubarb overnight in boiling water following the suggested amount below. I keep the rind on the watermelon for the visual impact but, by all means, remove it if you prefer.

Place all the ingredients into a large pitcher and add 1.8 litres (61 fl oz) water, stir together and store in the fridge at least 30 minutes before serving. Pour into glasses over ice, if you like.

ZA'ATAR & LEMON AQUA

makes   1.8 litres (61 fl oz)
prep   5 minutes,
           plus chilling time

handful za'atar leaves, lightly
   bruised (or handful thyme
   or oregano sprigs)
1 lemon, thinly sliced

Place all the ingredients into a large pitcher and add 1.8 litres (61 fl oz) water, stir together and store in the fridge at least 30 minutes before serving.

CAFÉ BLANC SPRITZER

makes   1.8 litres (61 fl oz)
prep   5 minutes,
           plus chilling time

1.8 litres (61 fl oz) sparkling
   water
1–2 tablespoons orange
   blossom water
1 orange or pink grapefruit,
   thinly sliced

Café blanc is a bit of a misnomer as it's not at all a coffee, nor white – it's an orange blossom tea, served as a digestive aid at the end of dinner. The drink is also the go-to home cure for anxiety, grief... and acne. In hot weather it can be reimagined as a chilled spritzer, as here.

Place all the ingredients into a large pitcher, stir together and store in the fridge at least 30 minutes before serving.

FROM SHAI TO QAHWA

Tea and coffee are ubiquitous in the Middle East. Both are popular and indispensible in hospitality, tradition, ceremony and celebrations. Tea or *shay* in Arabic is consumed anytime during the day in the Middle East. Coffee, on the other hand, while equally as popular, had a battle to win first.

Coffee was controversial. Considered unlawful or *haram* because of its intoxicating effects, it eventually won over even the strict religious fundamentalists by argument of its alerting effects on the pious. The Ottomans would eventually establish the first coffee house, and the spread of the brew would enter the European world.

The true etymology of 'coffee' is open for debate. It is generally agreed that the coffee plant itself was introduced into Yemen from its indigenous town of Kaffa in Ethiopia, which makes it a strong contender for the source of the word. However, is it a coincidence that coffee, which we know came via the Arabic *qahwa* by way of the Turkish *kahve*, sounds like 'coffee'? Or that the Arabic qahwa was an existing word already in use to mean 'wine'? This also explains the European attribution of coffee as the 'wine of Islam'.

Black tea is typical but many other teas are prepared and consumed for their medicinal properties. The most popular are *na'ana* (mint tea) – of course – *yansoun* (aniseed tea) and *zhoorat* (potpourri tea). Two others, among my favourites, follow.

ZA'ATAR & LAVENDER TEA

serves   4–6
prep   5 minutes

2 tablespoons fresh or
   dried za'atar leaves
1 teaspoon fresh or dried
   lavender
orange blossom honey, or
   honey of choice

I once asked Abu Kassem, a notable za'atar producer on my
Taste Lebanon tours, what the benefits of za'atar (the herb not the
condiment) were and he gave me a five-minute speech of its malady-
fighting properties. 'It cures all' he began... In any case, za'atar water,
whether hot or cold, is one of the oldest documented medicinal
remedies and is the first thing folk medicine suggests as a cure for
coughs and bronchitis. You can also use distilled za'atar water for
aromatherapy, as a natural antiseptic, as an anti-inflammatory and it's
great for an upset stomach. If you don't have za'atar leaves feel free to
use thyme or oregano sprigs instead.

Place the za'atar leaves and lavender into a teapot. Pour over 1 litre
(34 fl oz/4 cups) hot water and leave to brew for 5 minutes. Strain and
serve with honey to taste.

FENUGREEK TEA

serves   4–6
cook   10 minutes

1 tablespoon fenugreek
   seeds
pinch of ground nutmeg
2 tablespoons honey

Place the fenugreek seeds and nutmeg into a saucepan and add 1 litre
(34 fl oz/4 cups) water. Bring to a gentle simmer for about 5 minutes.
Remove from the heat and steep for 5 minutes. Strain and stir in the
honey. Serve.

ARAK & ZA'ATAR BLOODY MARYAM

serves   4
prep   5 minutes

1 heaping tablespoon Za'atar
   blend (page 84)
8 lemon or lime wedges
4 lime wedges, plus extra to
   garnish
230 ml (8 fl oz/scant 1 cup)
   arak or Pernod
470 ml (16 fl oz/scant 2 cups)
   tomato juice
6–8 dashes Tabasco sauce
6–8 dashes Worcestershire
   sauce
1 teaspoon celery salt or
   flaky sea salt
1 teaspoon freshly ground
   black pepper
1 teaspoon smoked paprika
3–4 tablespoons pickling
   brine, such as Rainbow
   torshi slaw brine (page 88)
ice cubes
fresh za'atar sprigs (or
   oregano, marjoram or
   thyme sprigs), to garnish
2 celery sticks, quartered,
   to garnish
olives, to garnish

Here, the anise flavouring in the arak finds a natural playmate with the tomato juice. Za'atar around the rim makes going back for another sip that bit more enticing. Adjust headiness to taste.

Scatter the za'atar blend onto a small plate. Rub the juicy side of a lemon or lime wedge along the rim of a tall glass then press the outer edge of the glass in the za'atar mixture until fully coated. Fill the glass with ice and set aside. Repeat with three more glasses.

Squeeze the remaining lemon and lime wedges into a cocktail shaker and drop them in. Add the remaining ingredients, fill with ice, then shake gently. Strain into the prepared glasses. Garnish with a sprig of herb and lime wedge, celery stick and olives.

ARABIC COFFEE

serves   4
prep   5 minutes
cook   5 minutes

1–2 teaspoons sugar
  (optional)
4 heaped teaspoons roasted
  and ground Arabic coffee
1 teaspoon Hawayej spice
  mix (page 28) (optional)
1 teaspoon rosewater
  (optional)

Arabic coffee, or *qahwah arabiyya*, does not relate to a particular Arabic coffee bean but rather the technique of preparing and infusing coffee, with spices such as cardamom, cloves and cinnamon, scented water, or saffron for a golden hue. The beans are roasted separately and then combined and ground together with the spices before being brewed, although sometimes the flavourings are added during brewing. You can purchase pre-ground, seasoned coffee. Sugar may also be added but traditionally the coffee is served black with dates.

Bring a saucepan of 275 ml (9½ fl oz) water to the boil. Add the sugar, if using, and heat gently to dissolve. Stir in the coffee, rosewater, if using, and let it simmer away gently until it starts to rise and foam or develop what is called a *raghwe*. As this rise occurs, remove the pan from the heat for 1 minute, then return to a low heat and simmer until the foam is reduced.

Take off the heat, transfer to a coffee pot, if you like, cover and leave to rest for a minute or two to allow the coffee grounds to settle. Pour, sharing the coffee across the cups in increments (this is to ensure everyone gets a taste of the raghwe), and never fill a cup more than three-quarters. The sediment at the bottom of the cup that one carefully avoids drinking is used for fortune telling (page opposite).

CODE OF TASTE

ada or morra	black or bitter coffee meaning no sugar added
ahweh helwe	sweetened
ahweh mazboot	right coffee meaning medium amount of sugar
ahweh ziyada	very sweet

AL TEBSEER

OR COFFEE GROUNDS READING FOR BEGINNERS

Simply swirl your coffee cup, make a wish and turn it
upside down on the saucer for a couple of minutes.
Someone else should do your reading.

If in the coffee grounds you see:

a heart
love is on the way

a nest
pregnancy

flowers
happiness will surround you

a ring
marriage

a fish
career achievement

a bird
good news

AL KOHL

Today, alcohol is still considered *haram* (illegal) in most Middle Eastern countries, though there are exceptions. The Levant takes pride in its multitude of boutique vineyards and distilleries where wine and arak – one of the first liqueurs (page 57) – have a rich heritage. Both were believed to have been developed by Christian and Jewish minorities in the valleys and mountains of modern-day Syria and Lebanon, where grapes were sweet and plentiful.

While the debate on whether Islam does literally prohibit alcohol continues, the ban itself seems to have come about gradually. In early Islam, drinking was so widespread among Muslims that it threatened to destabilise the Caliphate. But once in place, the ban was perhaps the reason why the Caliphate's armies were able to defeat their (drunken) enemies in battle, furthering the Islamic empire (though the Ottomans would power their janissaries with the low-alcohol *boza*, page 57).

Although drinks like *sharabs* (page 244), such as *jallab* (page 57) became the pour of the day, prohibition did not completely turn the tap off fermented drinks such as *mashroub* or *khamr* (wine). And, despite the religious disapproval, wine became celebrated within wealthy social and literary circles, flowing heavily within Sufi poetry and *belle lettres* of the time. It was even prescribed as medicine.

While fermented drinks in the region are as old as bread, the distillation of alcohol would come with the invention of the alembic pot, or still, by a Muslim chemist in the eighth century called Abu Musa Jabir ibn Hayyan aka Jabir. As Islam had by now a very strict prohibition in place, the Arabs used the invention not for alcohol but rather to distill perfumes, as well as eyeliner or *kohl*. They carried the art of distilling kohl to Spain from where it spread to the rest of Europe. The transition to liqueur production ensued. The Arabic name *al-kohl*, would be adopted, becoming 'alcohol' and refer to spirits and fermented drinks in the Arab world too.

So, let's raise a glass to Jabir and, as we say in Arabic, 'keskoun'!

JALLAB MOCKTAIL

serves 4
prep   5 minutes

12 tablespoons jallab syrup
4 teaspoons rosewater
  (optional)
crushed ice
4 tablespoons golden raisins
4 tablespoons pine nuts

Sharab is the term for soft drinks, and this one can be considered the Middle East's virgin Long Island Iced Tea. Jallab syrup, used to make this drink, is treacle-sweet and made from dates, carob and grape molasses that have been smoked with incense. The drink is a refreshing taste of the breezy east Mediterranean summers. Here's a recipe using ready-made jallab syrup. Make sure you seek out a high-quality brand such as Mymoune. See picture opposite.

Combine the jallab syrup and rosewater, if using, with cold water in a carafe.

Add as much crushed ice as you like and then top the drink with the raisins and pine nuts.

MINT & ORANGE BLOSSOM LEMONADE FIZZ

serves 6–8
prep   5 minutes

5–6 lemons, zest of 2 and
  juice yielding about 250 ml
  (8½ fl oz/1 cup)
handful mint leaves
5 tablespoons sugar or
  honey, or to taste
1 tablespoon orange
  blossom water
about 750 ml (25½ fl oz/
  3 cups) sparkling water
ice cubes

If you're after a Lebanese party vibe, spike the fizz with arak (page 57) or Pernod.

Add the lemon zest and juice to a carafe. Crush or pound the mint leaves with the sugar (if using) using a mortar and pestle, then add to the lemon juice. Stir in the orange blossom water, honey (if using) and the sparkling water. Taste and adjust the sweetness accordingly. Add ice to individual glasses and serve.

FOGGY MEADOW

serves 4–8
prep   10 minutes,
        plus freezing time

small handful (2–4 leaves
  or sprigs of each) of fresh
  herbs and edible flowers
  (such as borage flowers,
  calendula, rose petals,
  chicory flowers, lavender,
  basil, rosemary, za'atar
  leaves, pomegranate
  seeds, berries)
225 ml (8 fl oz) arak
  or Pernod

The Middle East's anise-flavoured liqueur par excellence, arak, is nicknamed the 'milk of lions' due to the cloudy white fog that develops when it is mixed with water. The lion association probably relates to the potency of the drink and the fearless behaviour one might entertain once sozzled! Arak is popular around the region – it's called ouzo in Greece, raki in Turkey and araki in Iran – though not all are made equal. The arak of Iraq, for example, is made of dates not grapes. Arak is the drink of choice for mezze, as it works as a digestive and a palate cleanser and suits the leisurely and varied spreads.

Foggy meadow is simply very pretty ice cubes to serve with arak. The ice should never be added first as this causes a film to appear on the liquid, which is why arak is always mixed with water in a carafe before pouring. See picture opposite.

Bring 300 ml (10 fl oz) water to the boil in a saucepan and simmer for 5–7 minutes to allow it to release the air, which will ensure clear ice cubes. Leave to cool to room temperature. Add a few herbs or flowers face down into each recess of your ice cube tray. Pour in the cooled water and freeze until solid.

To fill a 750 ml (25½ fl oz/3 cup) carafe, mix the arak with 525 ml (17½ fl oz) water. Pour into small glasses and add 2–3 ice cubes to each.

BRINE FOR LIFE ARAKTINI

serves 4
prep   5 minutes

80 ml (2½ fl oz/⅓ cup) arak
80 ml (2½ fl oz/⅓ cup) dry
  vermouth
340 ml (11½ fl oz/1⅓ cups)
  pickling brine (such as
  from the Turnip & beetroot
  ombre pickle, page 92)
ice cubes
4–8 spiky za'atar leaves
1 dried lime, finely crushed

Pickle juice is held in high regard in the Middle East and Turkey in particular where specialty stores sell pickles and pickle juice such as boza and *salgam*. Salgam is made from fermented turnips, carrots and burghul. Traditionally, it's served alongside *raki* to contrast the flavour and as a preventative measure for hangovers. Boza, the root word perhaps of booze, is similar, and while not made with brine, it is based on fermented burghul, which yields one per cent alcohol.

I prefer the simpler *tursu suyu*, the mouth-puckering brine of pickled veggies. Keep the lovely brine from the pickles you've made (page 92) – it's the key to a great martini.

Arak makes a refreshingly heady contender. I offered the 'araktini' recipe to my friend and blogger Najib Mitri, which was featured in magazines in the region and now it seems the name has caught on.

In a cocktail shaker, add the arak, vermouth, brine and ice and shake well. Divide between martini glasses and add a few za'atar leaves. Sprinkle the top with a pinch of the crushed lime.

3

DECORATE THE TABLE

CRUDITÉS, CANAPÉS AND PRET-A-MANGER

SET THE SOFRA

Zayneh el sofra or literally 'decorate the table' is what I grew up hearing in anticipation of meals. Presentation is always an essential element. Whether a cloth laid out on the floor, a low tray or high lavish table, the sofra is adorned with its edible ornaments before guests begin to arrive. Although the dishes served will vary, the act of gathering around a hospitable table is a central part of life across the region.

Show up to any Middle Eastern home and watch the host jewel the table out of nowhere. How do they do it? Vigilance. The freezer will always be filled with pret-a-manger foods also known as *hawader*, encompassing Kebbeh (page 122), Fatayer (page 116), topped flatbreads (page 112), you name it. More cardinal to the jewelled table, is the pantry, traditionally homes have a whole chamber (*oudet el mouneh*) designated in its honour. Its yearly winter provisions are prepared in a beautiful ritual. Crates of freshly harvested produce in hand and Kilner (Mason) jars on their stovetops undergoing fervid sterilisation, women of the household or village come together in a chatter to preserve the season's bounty. Pickles and preserved vegetables (pages 85, 88 and 92), aged yoghurt (pages 97–105) and fermented dips, olives, relishes and condiments, kick-back on the shelf to embrace time.

From pickled salads, simmered sauces to fermented grains, ahead you'll find some incredible preparations that are essential to any pantry and to decorate a table for breakfast, lunch, dinner or last-minute gatherings. The next time someone knocks on your door, a spontaneous but very jewelled table might manage to come together almost effortlessly.

LA'EENE WALA TA3MEENE

'WELCOME ME RATHER THAN FEED ME'

The gist: 'I'd rather taste your enthusiasm and excitement for hosting me, than what you're actually going to feed me.' Although part of a host's welcome is gauged through their food offerings, it also extends to encompass their warmth, engagement and treatment of their guests.

DON'T SPILL THE SALT:

The people of our combined past had awe-inspiring wisdom, as seen through the architecture and engineering they left behind. But perhaps their most persistent legacy lies in the ancient food-processing technologies. As the old saying goes, 'necessity is the mother of invention'. Along with trial and error and some serendipity, our ancestors overcame hunger while providing us some of our most celebrated foods and techniques.

Salt or *milh* was the world's first and most important condiment, but salt was also the original food processor, helping us transform basic ingredients into an array of delicacies. Salt has given us pickles, relishes, cheese, cured meats, sauces and salsas (yes, very popular to the Middle East, see pages 76, 77 and 79) and the world of salad.

Allegedly hailed by the Prophet Muhammad as 'the lord of condiments', in the ancient world, salt was the most valuable commodity on earth. Not only could it enhance the flavour of food and prolong its shelf-life but it was essential to human survival. So crucial to everyday life, salt became a symbol of hospitality, friendship and loyalty. The Middle Eastern saying 'there is bread and salt between us' speaks to the enduring value of salt in preserving an alliance once such hospitality has been shared. Welcoming someone with salt and bread at the table was an offer of friendship, and accepting someone's salt was a vow of loyalty. This, in turn, is why it was so unlucky to spill the salt on the table since you would be breaking that bond and disrespecting everything it represented.

Traditional acts such as salting, drying, oil-packing, pickling, smoking, sun-drying, basting in honey, refrigerating in caves and under cold water and even cooking (food processing in its most original form) are all inherited food engineering technologies. Yet this ancient wisdom was falling into neglect with the onset of industrialisation. We seem to be realising now that it's foolish to turn our backs on millennia of sophisticated and logical – and delicious – traditions. What the modernising industrial world missed was that the ancients were so advanced in their food processing that they were not only ahead of their time but ours, too.

DUKKAH SALT

makes   about 100 g
        (3½ oz/1 cup)
prep   10 minutes

½ teaspoon fennel seeds
1 teaspoon coriander seeds
1 teaspoon caraway seeds
½ teaspoon cumin seeds
65 g (2½ oz) flaky sea salt
handful toasted macadamia
    nuts, crushed (optional)

We tend to dip bread, raw vegetables and green pulses, such as fresh broad beans (fava beans), straight into plain or seasoned salt. The following seasoned salts would do nicely paired with a mixed vegetable platter (page 75). You can also use it sprinkled over hummus or as a dry rub for meat. It can be stored on your kitchen counter and used to season dishes as you go or as a final seasoning, to your liking. You can take it a step further – as I do – and keep some tucked away in a small portable jar in your purse.

Toast all the seeds in a pan over medium-high heat for about 3 minutes, stirring constantly. Remove from the heat, transfer to a plate and allow to cool completely.

When the ingredients have cooled, transfer to a spice grinder or food processor. Add the salt. Pulse all ingredients together until roughly the size of breadcrumbs. Don't over-process the mixture – stop when it's still dry and coarse. Combine with the macadamia nuts, if using. Serve with bread and good extra virgin olive oil. Keeps for up to 6 months in an airtight container in a cool, dark place.

MILH MUZ'ATAR

ZA'ATAR & LAVENDER SALT

makes   about 65 g (2½ oz/
        ⅓ cup)
prep   10 minutes

65 g (2½ oz) flaky sea salt
1 tablespoon dried and
    ground za'atar (or a mix of
    ground thyme, marjoram or
    oregano)
1 tablespoon dried lavender,
    lightly crushed
2 tablespoons ground sumac

This is based on a medieval recipe mentioned in Al warraq's *Kitab al Tabikh* – a medieval cookbook from Baghdad – and perhaps the very precursor of today's more za'atar-centric ubiquitous blend (see also page 85). In any case, the lavender here is a wonderful addition. Try this used in place of za'atar blend, where needed, to get that addictive za'atar taste without compromise. It can be stored on your kitchen counter and used to season dishes as a final seasoning or kept on the table for everyone to add to their liking.

Combine all the ingredients in a bowl. Serve with bread and extra virgin olive oil. Keep in a salt house on the kitchen table or transfer to an airtight jar and store in a cool, dark place for up to a year.

GOING BIZR-K: NUTS, SEEDS & OTHER NIBBLES

Nibbling on *bzoorat* (singular, *bizr*) or seeds and nuts is an actual pastime in the Middle East. 'Seeding' quickly evokes an image of elderly men sitting around a game of backgammon, circled by their seed-eating remnants, or a taxi driver chewing away with one arm out the window, or simply my own time spent seeding while watching telly or during cocktail-drinking bonanzas. Favoured as snacks, they are equally delicious tossed over salads and dips.

POMEGRANATE & CUMIN CASHEWS

makes   150 g (5½ oz/1 cup)
prep   20 minutes
cook   20 minutes

150 g (5½ oz/1 cup) raw
  (unsalted) cashews
1 teaspoon ground cumin
½ teaspoon Aleppo pepper
  flakes or dried chilli flakes
1 tablespoon pomegranate
  molasses
1 teaspoon olive oil
2 teaspoons honey
1 teaspoon fine sea salt

Preheat the oven to 150°C/300°F/Gas 2. Line a baking tray with baking (parchment) paper.

Toss the cashews with the cumin, Aleppo pepper, pomegranate molasses, oil, honey and salt in a bowl to combine. Spread the cashews on the prepared tray and bake for 20 minutes, turning halfway through the cooking time, until golden. Serve slightly warm or at room temperature. The nuts keep in an airtight container in a cool, dark place for 1–2 weeks.

ORANGE BLOSSOM HONEY PISTACHIOS

makes   200 g (7 oz/
             1½ cups)
prep   20 minutes
cook   20 minutes

200 g (7 oz/1½ cups)
  unsalted shelled pistachios
1 tablespoon honey
pinch of ground cinnamon
1 tablespoon orange
  blossom water
1 tablespoon melted butter

Preheat the oven to 150°C/300°F/Gas 2. Line a baking tray with baking (parchment) paper.

Toss the ingredients in a bowl to combine. Spread the pistachios on the prepared baking tray and bake for 20 minutes, turning halfway through the cooking time, or until golden. Serve slightly warm or at room temperature. The nuts keep in an airtight container in a cool, dark place for 1–2 weeks.

HAWAYEJ SPICED TOASTED CHICKPEAS

makes   200 g (7 oz)
prep   soaking time
        (if using dried
        chickpeas)
cook   1 hour 15 minutes
        if using dried
        chickpeas,
        30 minutes if using
        tinned

200 g (7 oz) dried chickpeas
    or 350 g (12 oz) tinned
    chickpeas, drained
    and rinsed
1 tablespoon Hawayej spice
    mix (page 28)
1 teaspoon smoked sea salt,
    plus more to taste
1 tablespoon olive oil

Preheat the oven to 200°C/400°F/Gas 6.

Soak the chickpeas in water overnight. The next day, place in a saucepan with fresh water and bring to the boil over high heat. Reduce the heat to medium and simmer for 30–45 minutes, until tender. Drain very well.

Make sure the cooked or tinned chickpeas are very dry and pat with paper towels if needed. In a bowl, toss the chickpeas in the hawayej spice mixture and salt.

Brush a baking tray with the oil, spread over the chickpeas and bake for about 15 minutes. Remove from the oven, shake to redistribute and then bake for a further 15 minutes. Remove and leave to cool for 10 minutes. Serve warm or at room temperature. The chickpeas keep in an airtight container in a cool, dark place for 1–2 weeks.

TEA TOWEL POPCORN

WITH KISHK

makes   4 bowls
prep   5 minutes
cook   5 minutes

2 tablespoons rapeseed oil
100 g (3½ oz) popcorn
   kernels
30 g (1 oz) Aged butter (page
   27) or clarified butter,
   (optional)
flaky sea salt or seasoned
   salt of choice (page 67)
1 tablespoon kishk flour
   (page 101) (optional)

If you choose, you can replace the aged butter with regular butter, although the flavour of the former does shine here. I find a dusting of kishk works well in adding that umami flavour. The tea towel helps absorb the moisture and makes for a crisp pop.

Place a large pan over medium heat, pour in the oil, allow to heat through for a few seconds, then add the popcorn. Wrap the lid of the pan in a clean tea towel and tie it into a tight knot at the handle, then cover the saucepan with the lid as tightly as you can so that any steam does not escape. (The tea towel will prevent the moisture from dripping into the pan and making the popcorn soggy.) Allow the popcorn to pop, shaking the pan gently every so often. Once you hear the popping reduce to one pop every 10 seconds, remove from the heat.

Meanwhile, melt the butter then drizzle it over the popped corn, sprinkle over the salt and, if using, the kishk flour to taste. Shake well, and serve in individual serving bowls or in a large one.

PLATED GARDENS

& UNDRESSED SALADS

An assortment of fresh and pickled vegetables and herbs is essential and even a centrepiece to a Middle Eastern table. *Sabzi khordan*, or 'eating greens', as is said in Farsi, and *sahn khodra* or 'vegetable platter' as is said in Arabic, is a way of life for the people of the region, carnivores included. The platters of mixed greens and seasonal vegetables are often served undressed and with an accompanying knife to give the guests freedom to prepare and eat as they wish. They are enjoyed as appetisers or as sides to a more substantial main meal, alongside dips. In the Levant, it's popular to serve heirloom tomatoes as part of the vegetable platter, and you will likely see one of the diners slicing the tomato and seasoning it with some whipped garlic aioli and a sprinkling of sumac or simply salt, olive oil and torn mint before passing the plate around for all to share.

A vegetable platter can be simple, substantial or a visual masterpiece.

HERE ARE A FEW SUGGESTIONS OF TRADITIONAL SERVINGS:

- Herbs and seasonal greens: soft herbs such as mint, tarragon, parsley, basil, chives or dill.

- Cheese such as halloumi, feta, aged labneh (page 24), green kishk (page 104).

- An array of seasonal vegetables such as heirloom tomatoes, peas, broad beans (fava beans), carrots, cucumber, radish and spring onions, and cured olives.

- Canapé-style: insert toothpicks into cheese cubes or labneh balls (page 97) or cherry tomatoes.

- Carrots cut into fingers and marinated in iced lemon juice, then sprinkled with salt. Soak cucumber slices in minty, iced water with seasoned salt.

SMOKED TOMATO HOT SAUCE

makes 3 x 250 ml
(8½ fl oz/
1 cup) jars
prep 20 minutes
cook 45 minutes

1.5 kg (3 lb 5 oz) tomatoes
125 g (4 oz) hot red chillies
4 tablespoons olive oil
1 large onion, finely chopped
2 garlic heads, cloves peeled
   and thinly sliced
1 tablespoon mustard seeds
4 tablespoons balsamic
   vinegar
flaky sea salt, to taste
olive oil, to cover

This Levantine hot sauce is the fiery cousin of harissa. I'm not the biggest fan of hot sauces, but this one keeps me coming back for more. *Shatta* means hot chilli, but you can adjust the heat level to taste by combining red peppers with the chillies. This will lend a sweeter note, too. It's definitely messier to char the tomatoes and chilli directly over your gas stovetop but I find the method most effective to get that much-needed smokiness. You can opt for a heavy-based griddle pan or a barbecue instead.

Place the tomatoes directly on the flame of a gas hob (depending on the size of your hob, you may be able to fit 2–3 tomatoes on each) or barbecue and char them for 5–6 minutes each, turning them halfway through, until blackened and beginning to peel. Repeat with the chillies. Alternatively, preheat the oven to 200°C/400°F/Gas 6. Place the tomatoes on one baking tray and the chillies on a separate one. Roast in the oven until blistered and blackened.

Transfer to a pan and cover with the lid. Set aside to steam while you cook the onions.

Heat the oil in a saucepan, add the onion and garlic and toss. Cover with the lid and allow them to sweat over very low heat for 15–20 minutes. Check them occasionally and stir to make sure they don't brown – essentially, you're looking to soften them until they are 'creamed' – and, if necessary, take the pan off the heat for a minute or so to control the temperature. (Add a little water to help minimise browning if necessary.) Add the mustard seeds and cook for a further 2–3 minutes.

While the onions are cooking, peel the skins from the tomatoes and remove the seeds, reserving any of the liquid. Roughly chop the tomatoes. Wipe or brush off the burnt skins from the chillies and then finely chop. Add the chillies to the onion mixture, toss to combine and then cook, uncovered, for 2–3 minutes. Pour over the vinegar, cook for 30 seconds, then using a hand blender, purée the mixture. Pour in the reserved tomato liquid and blitz again to form a smooth consistency. Return the pan to high heat, add the tomatoes, season to taste and bring to the boil. Cook for a further 10–15 minutes or until slightly thickened. I prefer my smoked tomato hot sauce on the chunkier side, so I don't cook the tomatoes for too long.

Transfer to sterilised jars and pour enough oil over the sauce to cover. Allow to cool slightly, then seal the jar and store in the fridge for up to 3 months. Make sure after each use to top up with oil to prolong shelf-life.

ZHUG SALSA

prep   5 minutes
makes   1 x 750 ml
        (25½ fl oz/
        3 cups) jar

3-4 fresh green chillies,
    halved
1 garlic head, cloves peeled
    and roughly chopped
large bunch (about 125 g/
    4 oz) coriander (cilantro),
    leaves and stalks
60 g (2 oz) parsley, leaves
    and stalks
½ onion, peeled
15 g (½ oz) piece ginger,
    peeled
1 teaspoon mustard seeds
juice of 1 lemon
1 heaped tablespoon flaky
    sea salt
250 ml (8½ fl oz/1 cup) olive
    oil, plus extra for covering

Here is my version of my Yemeni friend Shaima's go-to recipe. Shaima is adamant that everyone know the correct pronunciation to be '*sahoog*', meaning 'ground' (it's traditionally prepared on a slab of stone and crushed using a pestle). This 'salsa' is like a pesto and comes in various forms – some are red from the presence of red chillies others are brown from the addition of tomatoes. I prefer it green and rather mild as I'm not a fan of overpowering heat. This is completely under your control so adjust the amount of chilli to your liking. It is best served fresh with bread for dipping or slathered into wraps. Of course, as Shaima also proclaimed; 'No mandi session is complete without this condiment.' So, once you make it, go ahead and try the Dewy quail and mutton mandi (page 232).

Add everything except the oil to a blender or food processor. Pulse to form a paste. Add the oil and blitz again. Serve fresh or transfer to a sterilised jar and pour over some oil to cover. The salsa will keep in the fridge for up to 3 weeks.

IT'S ALL FENUGREEK TO ME

As a legume, herb and spice, multifaceted fenugreek has been celebrated throughout history. This culinary gem, native to the East Mediterranean, is beloved for its versatility, unique flavour profile as well as its health benefits. The flavour it imparts can be nutty, caramel-like, definitely heady, it unreservedly headlines anywhere it's added. Too much fenugreek can make your dish bitter, so a little goes a long way in terms of taste.

Fenugreek comes as seeds, ground seeds or leaves (used much in Iran and known as *shanbalile*) and makes for delicious seasoning of leafy greens and pulses, breads, dips, pickles and preserves. It is essential to curries and the classic Persian *sabzi* (herb) mix (see the Salmon feast, pages 226–227). The seeds can be soaked, sprouted and toasted then added to salads to provide a flavour-packed crunch (page 87). Ground fenugreek is also essential in various types of meat rubs in Armenia, notably in *basturma* where it also takes the form of a dip or paste, called *chemen*. In Yemen, it's the basis for helbeh (page 79) also its Arabic namesake. The Greeks boil the seeds for tea (page 47), and in Egypt and Palestine, it's used in a sweet cake (page 254).

FENUGREEK RELISH

makes 250 ml (8½ fl oz/
1 cup)
prep 10 minutes, plus
soaking time

1 tablespoon fenugreek
seeds
1 tablespoon tamarind
pulp or 2–3 tablespoons
tamarind juice
1 teaspoon flaky sea salt

This relish is traditionally served with Yemeni bread, which goes by the name *malawa* and *mandi* (page 232). If you'd like to jazz this up and serve it as a dip alongside bread, toss in a finely chopped garlic clove, or mix in a couple of tablespoons of the Zhug salsa (page 77) and a tablespoon or so of Smoked tomato hot sauce (page 76).

In a small deep bowl, dissolve the fenugreek seeds in 250 ml (8½ fl oz/ 1 cup) water and leave to sit for at least 1 hour or overnight (change the water once if you're able to). The longer the fenugreek soaks the less bitter the end result.

If using tamarind pulp, soak it in a bowl with about 60 ml (2 fl oz/¼ cup) warm water for 30 minutes. Stir the tamarind well to dissolve it into the water and strain, reserving the juice.

Next, strain off any excess water from the fenugreek water using a fine mesh strainer, then, using a hand blender, blitz for 5–8 minutes, or until white, creamy and frothy. Next, whisk in 2–3 tablespoons tamarind juice and the salt. Taste and adjust the seasoning. Keeps in the fridge for a couple of days.

CUCUMBER & MINT YOGHURT

serves   4–8
prep   5 minutes

175 g (6 oz) full-fat Greek
    yoghurt or soft labneh
    (page 25)
75 g (2½ oz) cucumber, grated
    or diced, plus extra slices
    to decorate
1 teaspoon dried mint
1 small garlic clove, very finely
    chopped (optional)
zest of ½ lemon
flaky sea salt

Combine the ingredients in a mixing bowl. Taste and adjust the seasoning and texture to your liking. Serve as a dip or condiment.

Also try: For another regional variation known as 'mesh', substitute the cucumber and mint for 75 g (2¾ oz/½ cup) crumbled feta, ½ teaspoon ground fenugreek, 1 finely chopped green chilli, a handful of chopped coriander (cilantro) leaves and 1 tablespoon nigella seeds.

UP CLOSE AND PERSONAL WITH ZA'ATAR

You may be familiar with 'za'atar', but perhaps, unless you've travelled to the Middle East, only as the herb-and-spice blend: ground za'atar (the herb), sumac, toasted sesame seeds and salt. There's more to za'atar than the blend. But nor is it a simple case of 'za'atar' meaning either the blend or the herb. In fact, a good deal of confusion reigns. Za'atar is the generic term used to describe a family of shrubby Middle Eastern plants, swaying between characteristics of oregano, marjoram, thyme and savory. Thriving in very hot, dry, rocky areas, za'atar has traditionally been a foraged perennial (*za'atar barre*). Now endangered in the wild, the cultivated form is more common.

There are two main varieties. The predominant za'atar (*Origanum syriacum*, and for our purposes, 'furry za'atar'), is a stubby-leaved variety with a spicy 'bite' when eaten fresh – though more subtle when dry – that shares warm notes of oregano, marjoram and thyme. It is this za'atar that is dried and ground to star in the za'atar blend. Common oregano is not at all the same as za'atar, which is why if you're attempting to make the blend in the West and without access to the 'real deal' then I suggest a combination of oregano, thyme and marjoram.

The second type of za'atar, *Thymbra spicata* (donkey hyssop and winter savory, or for our purposes 'spiked thyme'), is a long, slender, spiky but tender-leaf herb. It has a more mellow taste and is used in salads (page 84), to stuff pastries, in sandwiches, fried crisp and used as a topping, roasted with vegetables or as a pesto for pasta and in pickles (for example, curing olives).

Contrary to common misapprehension, in the Middle East za'atar –
the blend – while an icon of Levantine life, is not the pass-par-tout
'fairy dust' it has become in the West. Za'atar blend includes already
toasted sesame seeds so will easily overcook and add a bitter note
to the dish. In the Middle East the blend features mainly as a table
condiment. In Syria and Jordan there is a nerdy proliferation of
eclectically flavoured and colourful za'atar blends. Some combine
za'atar with spices such as cumin, caraway, fennel and coriander
seeds. Others opt for a higher dose of sumac (or pomegranate
molasses) yielding 'red za'atar'. Others even replace sesame seeds
with pine nuts or pistachios (Persian za'atar), or ground chickpeas
like the Egyptian counterpart known as dukkah.

If making your own blend, be sure to use not fresh but dried za'atar
(Origanum syriacum – furry za'atar). Furry za'atar becomes a
light olive green when dried and ground. If the taste is not coming
through as pungent, it's likely a combination of other za'atar and
non-indigenous herbs and even wheat! Wheat, used to fluff, is often
even listed as an ingredient, a tell-tale sign to drop the bag. Watch
out for citric acid in pre-bought blends. The usual souring agent
should be sumac, which will add a reddish hue to the green.

SPIKED ZA'ATAR SALAD

serves 4–6 as part of
a multi-course
menu
prep   7 minutes

1 large onion, thinly sliced
1–2 teaspoons ground sumac
2–3 handfuls spiked za'atar
  leaves, stems removed, or
  preserved za'atar leaves in
  brine, soaked in water for
  10 minutes then rinsed and
  drained
2–3 tablespoons cider
  vinegar
4–5 tablespoons olive oil
firm labneh (page 25) or
  feta (optional)
handful pomegranate seeds
  (optional)
flaky sea salt and freshly
  ground black pepper

Za'atar salad is a simple combination of the thin, long leaves of 'spiky za'atar' (Thymbra spicata, see 'Up close and personal with za'atar', pages 82–83) tossed with sliced onions, sumac and dressed with a cider vinaigrette. The slender leaves pack a spicy punch of flavour, sort of a combination of pepper, oregano and mint. Fresh za'atar leaves are available from late winter and can be enjoyed throughout the spring, which is when you may be able to find these in Middle Eastern speciality stores. If not, an alternative is to use the pickled variety but decrease the amount of vinegar. This is a delicious salad served with a glass of arak (page 57) and as part of a mezze spread.

Place the onion slices in a mixing bowl with the sumac and rub well to coat. Add the remaining ingredients and toss everything to combine. Taste and adjust the seasoning as you like.

ZA'ATAR BLEND

makes about 60g (2¼ oz/
1 heaped cup)
prep   11 minutes
cook   11 minutes

30 g (1 oz/¼ cup) sesame
  seeds
30 g (1 oz/¼ cup) dry furry
  za'atar leaves or ground
  equal parts combination
  of dried thyme, marjoram
  and oregano
1–2 tablespoons sumac
  (add more or less to taste)
1 teaspoon fine sea salt

Toast the sesame seeds in a heavy-based saucepan over a medium heat for 1 minute until golden and fragrant, shaking the pan often.

Combine all the ingredients and use as required. Store the remainder in an airtight container away in a cool, dark place for up to one year.

SPIKED ZA'ATAR & ALMOND PESTO

makes 1 x 300 ml
(10 fl oz) jar
prep 10 minutes

80 g (2¾ oz) fresh spiked
za'atar leaves, stems
removed, or preserved
za'atar leaves in brine,
soaked in water for
10 minutes then rinsed
and drained
2–3 garlic cloves, roughly
chopped
10 g (½ oz) piece ginger,
peeled
3 preserved lemon wedges,
rinsed and seeds discarded
15 g (½ oz) pine nuts
15 g (½ oz) blanched
almonds, toasted (page 27)
60 ml (2 fl oz/ ¼ cup)
olive oil

Delicious on almost anything: *moghrabieh* (pearl couscous), a stuffing
for shish barak or breads and pastries, potatoes, roast vegetables,
chicken and so on. Grate over with jameed if you have any, or a
lovely pecorino.

If using jarred leaves, drain well. Add the garlic, ginger and za'atar
leaves to a food processor and blitz to a fine purée, about 2–3 minutes
depending on the power of your motor and sharpness of your blade.
Add the preserved lemon wedges and nuts, and blitz for a further
1–2 minutes until you reach a smooth consistency. Pour in 50 ml
(1¾ fl oz) oil and mix with a fork to combine.

Transfer to a jar and pour over the remaining oil to cover. Secure with the
lid and store in the fridge. It can be kept for up to 7 days once opened.

SALATA ARABIYA

QUICK-PICKLED ARABIC SALATA
WITH SPROUTED FENUGREEK

serves 6–8
prep 10 minutes, plus
sprouting time

2 tablespoons fenugreek
seeds
3–4 small cucumbers, or
½ regular cucumber, diced
2–3 tomatoes, diced
1 yellow (bell) pepper, diced
1–2 large shallots (about
150 g/5½ oz) thinly sliced
1 celery stalk, diced
20 olives, pitted and
roughly chopped
handful parsley leaves,
roughly chopped
handful mint leaves,
roughly chopped
1 small garlic clove, peeled
125 ml (5 fl oz/½ cup) cider
vinegar
60 ml (2 fl oz/¼ cup)
olive oil
1 tablespoon ground sumac
flaky sea salt and freshly
ground black pepper

This is the kind of salad that is best prepared up to an hour before
serving to give the ingredients a chance to macerate. The brine is
heavenly and I recommend drinking a little. Serve it with the Salmon
feast (pages 226–227) and toss with mixed seasonal green leaves and
Aysh pita pyramids (page 31) for a delicious fattoush.

A day or two before you want to make this salad, sprout the fenugreek
seeds by soaking them in a bowl with plenty of warm water and cover
for 4–5 hours. Drain, rinse well, then spread them on a large glass or
ceramic baking dish and moisten with a little warm water. Cover loosely
with a damp tea towel. Leave to sit for 1–2 days, until sprouted.

In a large mixing bowl, combine the cucumbers, tomatoes, pepper,
shallots, celery, olives and herbs. Finely grate over the garlic clove and
pour over the vinegar and oil, then season with sumac, salt and pepper.
Toss it all together very well to coat with the sprouted fenugreek, taste
and adjust seasoning.

RAINBOW TORSHI SLAW

makes   1 x 3 litre
         (101 fl oz) jar
prep   20 minutes, plus
         preserving time

for the brine:
1.5 litres (51 fl oz/6 cups)
    water
120 g (4½ oz) coarse salt

1 teaspoon white
    peppercorns
½ teaspoon black
    peppercorns
2 teaspoons coriander seeds
1 tablespoon mustard seeds
350 g (12½ oz) yellow squash,
    cut into matchsticks
125 g (4 oz) turnip, cut into
    matchsticks
350 g (12½ oz) red or green
    (bell) peppers, cut into
    matchsticks
300 g (10½ oz) kohlrabi, cut
    into matchsticks
350 g (12½ oz) carrots, cut
    into matchsticks
1 garlic head, cloves
    separated, unpeeled
½ onion, thinly sliced
60 g (2 oz) ginger, peeled
    and cut into fine
    matchsticks
2–3 vine leaves or bay leaves
2–3 tarragon sprigs

Torshi makhlout is a pickled salad – the original Mason (Kilner) jar salad really. I make this with whatever vegetables are in season and it never ceases to be a crowd pleaser. Vine leaves or other tannin-rich variants (such as bay leaves, cloves or even black tea leaves, but go easy) are essential to help the vegetables hold their crisp texture.

Make the brine. In a large pot, combine the water and salt and bring to a boil over medium-high heat. Stir to dissolve the salt. Set aside to cool.

Combine the spices in a small mixing bowl.

You can pack it two ways: layer in the vegetables according to colour as per below or toss all the vegetables in a large bowl and then pack into the jar. I prefer the former as it makes a beautiful display.

Layer according to colour. Start with reds, then orange, then yellow, green and finally purples. Between each colour, sprinkle in a few cloves of garlic, the onion, ginger and spice mix. Pack it all down. Add the vine leaves and tarragon sprigs and pour over the brine. Don't fully seal the jar, leave it open so it can breathe, anywhere from 2–3 days. Close it and shake once each day and then open it slightly to breathe. Seal and store in a dark place for 7–10 days. Once opened, keep it in the fridge. It keeps for at least 90 days.

Also try: To make an overnight version, sprinkle the vegetables with 1 tablespoon sea salt, massage to combine and leave for 10 minutes to allow the juices to develop. Skip making the brine and combine 60 ml (2 fl oz/¼ cup) cider vinegar with 1–2 teaspoons honey, then pour this over the vegetables. Transfer to a jar and pop into the fridge overnight. It's ready to eat the following day.

BABY AUBERGINES

STUFFED WITH GARLIC, WALNUT & POMEGRANATE

makes   3 x 700 ml
          (23½ fl oz) jars
prep   45 minutes, plus
          preserving time

2 kg (4 lb 6 oz) baby
  heirloom aubergines
  (eggplants)
4 garlic heads, cloves
  separated and peeled
1 tablespoon coarse sea salt
15 g (½ oz) coriander
  (cilantro), finely chopped
seeds of ½ pomegranate
120 g (4½ oz/1 cup) walnuts
  or pecans, finely chopped
540 ml (18 fl oz) olive oil
1–3 fresh red chillies, thinly
  sliced (optional)

These stuffed baby aubergines are so addictive, and amazing to have on hand in the pantry for showing off your last-minute hosting skills. Look for aubergines that are firm to the touch with a shiny skin. The quantity may seem large, but believe me, they won't last you the year. I once consumed so many straight from the jar in a daydream, only to realise I had dripped olive oil and stuffing all over my brand new silk blouse. While you can often find these baby aubergines in large supermarkets, the tiniest of them are at Middle Eastern grocers. Enjoy, but don't even think of sending me your dry cleaning bill!

Begin by peeling the green stems off the aubergines, leaving the bottom root as is. Place the aubergines in a steamer and steam for 5–10 minutes, until they have slightly softened. Alternatively, bring a saucepan of water to the boil and simmer them for the same amount of time.

Transfer the aubergines to a colander and leave them to drain and cool completely for about 30 minutes.

Using a knife, cut small vertical slits in the middle of the aubergines. Return them to the colander, set a weight such as a heavy bowl or plate on top and leave overnight. You can stack a few plates to apply additional pressure – this is to squeeze out any excess moisture from the aubergines.

The next day, prepare the stuffing. Blitz the garlic and salt in a food processor (or use a mortar and pestle) to form a fine paste. Add the coriander and pulse again until combined. Transfer to a serving bowl. Stir in the pomegranate seeds, walnuts and 45 ml (1½ fl oz) oil and mix well.

Take the strained aubergines and gently work the incisions open. Stuff each slit with about 1 teaspoon of the filling and then pack them into a sterilised jar, layering in the chilli slices, if using. Invert the jars at an angle onto a plate (lean them onto a small ramekin at the plate's centre) and leave to sit for a few hours to allow any remaining juices to seep out. Now flip the jars back upright and pour in the remaining oil. Use a spoon to gently wiggle the aubergines, allowing the oil to evenly cover them. Add more oil, if needed, to ensure all of the aubergines are covered. Wipe the rim with a clean, damp cloth. Tightly twist on the lid and store in a cool, dry place for 5 days. Serve at room temperature. Keeps for up to a year unopened and then 6 months in the fridge.

VINTAGE GARLIC
(OR NOT SO VINTAGE)

makes   1 x 250 ml
        (8½ fl oz/1 cup) jar
prep   10 minutes, plus
        preserving time

about 4 garlic heads, or
  enough to tightly pack a jar
60 ml (2 fl oz/¼ cup)
  balsamic vinegar
125 ml (4 fl oz/½ cup) cider
  vinegar, plus extra if
  needed
2 tablespoons honey
1 teaspoon sea salt
1 tablespoon dried
  barberries or cranberries
1–2 cloves
½ teaspoon coriander seeds

In Iran, raw garlic cloves immersed in vinegar for seven years or even longer are known as *torshi seer*. The longer they mature, the more delicious they become – think meltingly soft, like roast garlic but with sweet and sour tones; a sort of balsamic caramel. The colour develops from white ivory to blue-green, then finally fades to a golden mahogany brown. They last forever, so if you're going to make them, feel free to double the quantity. They are excellent enjoyed as they are or try adding them to stews, salads or marinades for a garlicky note.

Leave the garlic heads unpeeled but clean them of any fur and discard any excess fall-away peel. Pack them into a sterilised jar.

In a mixing bowl, combine the vinegars, honey and salt, and stir to dissolve. Pour the mixture into the jar to completely immerse the garlic, leaving about 2.5 cm (1 in) from the rim of the jar. You may need to add more vinegar to ensure the garlic is submerged.

Place the lid on the jar and twist to close but do not seal tightly. Leave to ferment for 2 days, loosening the lid to release gases twice a day. Each time, close the lid and shake the jar. Alternatively, use a jar fitted with an airlock. On the third day the garlic will have softened and should no longer float. Top up with a little vinegar to ensure they are submerged and reseal the jar. Store in a cool, dark place for at least a month before consuming. It keeps for 7 years.

TURNIP & BEETROOT OMBRE PICKLE

serves 8–10
makes   1 x 1.5 litre
        (51 fl oz/6 cup) jar
prep   10 minutes

75 g (2¾ oz) coarse sea salt
500 g (1 lb 2 oz) turnip, sliced
  into thin circles
200 g (7 oz) beetroot
  (beets), sliced into circles
2–3 spiked za'atar leaves or
  oregano or thyme sprigs
1–2 bay leaves

Cut the vegetables into any shape you like. I love them in thin shaved circles as they look great in a salad or as a garnish. Layer with avocado, crumbled aged labneh (page 25), more za'atar leaves or za'atar pesto (page 87) and a generous drizzle of olive oil.

Bring 750 ml (25½ fl oz/3 cups) water to the boil in a saucepan, then stir in the salt until dissolved. Leave to cool completely.

Layer in the turnip and beetroot slices, alternating the two, in a sterilised jar. Pour over the cooled brine, then add the leaves. Place in the fridge to ferment for 7 days before eating. It keeps for up to 1 month.

Also try: For a quick variation, place the turnip, beetroot and about 4–5 tablespoons cider vinegar in a glass jar. Shake well and leave to marinate for at least 4 hours or overnight.

BACON BASTURMA

makes 1.3 kg (2 lb 10 oz)
prep 1 hour,
plus curing
and drying

1 kg (2 lb 3 oz) coarse salt
600 g (1 lb 5 oz) soft light
brown sugar
1 x 2 kg (4 lb 6 oz) boneless
pork belly or beef
tenderloin

for the spice paste:
55 g (2 oz) paprika
90 g (3 oz) ground fenugreek
2½ tablespoons ground
coriander
2 tablespoons garlic powder
¾ teaspoon Aleppo pepper
flakes or dried chilli flakes
¾ teaspoon ground black
pepper
¾ teaspoon ground cumin
¾ teaspoon ground allspice

Basturma is a cured, heavily spiced, air-dried beef prominent in the Levant and Balkans. The Arabic 'basturma' derives from Turkish, where the root word originally meant 'to press' and then 'to preserve'. It's believed that the horsemen of Central Asia used to preserve meat by placing slabs of it wrapped in a thick paste of spices in an inner pocket of their saddles, where it would be pressed by their legs as they rode. Pastrami has its root in the same Turkish word, albeit via Romanian Yiddish. Basturma is likely inherited from the Byzantines, where it was known as *apokt*, which derives from the ancient language Parthian of north-eastern Iran, and means 'uncooked'. In Armenia this root word is still retained and the name for the meat is *aboukhd*. Winter is the ideal time to cure basturma, and it will take a good few days so patience is key.

In a mixing bowl, combine the salt and sugar. Line a wire rack with 3–4 sheets of greaseproof paper and place in a shallow baking tin. Add half the salt and sugar mixture to the lined rack and place the pork on top. Cover with the remaining salt and sugar mixture, making sure to thoroughly rub it into the meat. Lay another 3 sheets of greaseproof paper over the meat and weigh down with something heavy (such as a heavy book). Transfer to the centre of the fridge (to avoid any ice, which will add moisture and therefore rot your meat), and leave to cure for 5 days. If using beef, allow to cure for 3 days. On the final day of the cure, discard the blood and rinse the meat to remove the cure. Transfer to a large container and cover with plenty of water. Leave to soak for at least 2 hours, preferably overnight.

Remove the meat from the water and pat dry thoroughly using paper towels. Return the meat to a clean rack secured over a baking tin, cover ever so lightly with muslin (cheesecloth) or greaseproof paper, and leave to air-dry (if cool) in a semi-humid space or in the fridge for a further 48–72 hours.

On the final day of curing, combine the spices in a mixing bowl with 125–145 ml (4 fl oz/½ cup–5 fl oz) water to make a spreadable yet relatively dry paste. Remove the cured pork from the tin and unwrap. Spread the spice mixture all over the meat, making sure it's completely coated. Transfer to the centre of the fridge, wrap with a muslin cloth or pierce the meat and then add a kitchen thread to hang it to dry, wrapped in a muslin cloth in a very clean, dry and semi-humid space for 1 month. After that, store covered in greaseproof paper in an airtight container for up to 1 month.

LABNEH THREE WAYS

LABNEH MALBOUDEH
LAVENDER PEPPER LABNEH POPS

Labneh malboudeh refers to labneh that has been strained to a dry crumb, usually up to 3 days (see page 25), and then rolled into balls. These labneh balls, which come with a kitchen sink of other names (*labneh mzaazleh, labneh mdaableh, labneh mkaabeh, labneh kurat*) are either plain or tossed in seasoning and preserved in olive oil. The usual flavour contenders are mint, chilli or za'atar.

makes   250 g (9 oz)
        (serves 6-8 as part
        of a multi-course
        menu)
prep   10-15 minutes,
        plus straining time

250 g (9 oz) firm labneh
  (page 2)
3 tablespoons almond oil or
  olive oil, plus extra to cover
2 tablespoons orange
  blossom honey, or honey
  of choice

for the lavender pepper
2 teaspoons black or mixed
  peppercorns
1 teaspoon dried lavender
1 teaspoon fennel seeds
1 teaspoon Aleppo pepper
  flakes or dried chilli flakes
1 teaspoon dried tarragon
1 teaspoon ground allspice

To make the lavender pepper, place the spices in a spice grinder and pulse a couple of times, or until you have the texture of sand. Alternatively, use a mortar and pestle.

Sprinkle about 2 tablespoons of the lavender pepper on a plate. Roll the labneh to form small balls and then into the lavender pepper.

Transfer to a serving plate and drizzle over the oil and honey. Insert decorative toothpicks into each ball. Alternatively, transfer to a sterilised jar and pour over enough oil to cover the balls completely. Seal with the lid and store in the fridge for a month or longer.

LABNEH MFATEFTEH

DATE, MINT & PISTACHIO LABNEH CRUMBLE

makes   250 g (9 oz)
        (serves 6–8 as part
        of a multi-course
        menu)
prep   10 minutes

250 g (9 oz) firm labneh
  (page 28)
2 tablespoons pistachios,
  toasted and finely chopped
1 tablespoon dried mint
50 g (1¾ oz) pitted dates,
  finely chopped
1–2 tablespoons Argan oil
  or extra virgin olive oil,
  for serving

This is equally delicious using soft labneh, in which case you can fold in the listed ingredients and serve drizzled with oil of choice, or create a well in the centre of the labneh and then add the ingredients to it with oil drizzled over.

Crumble the labneh in a bowl. Add the pistachios, mint and dates and stir to combine. Serve as a starter alongside the vegetable platter on page 75 and some Mini Arabic bread puffs (page 30).

LABNEH B TOUM

WILD GARLIC LABNEH

makes   250 g (9 oz)
        (serves 6–8 as part
        of a multi-course
        menu)
prep   10 minutes

250 g (9 oz) soft labneh
generous handful of wild
  garlic, finely chopped (or
  3–4 peeled garlic cloves of
  choice, minced)
10 fresh mint leaves, finely
  chopped
1 teaspoon flaky sea salt
olive oil, to serve

Wild garlic, labneh and mint come together to make a typical levantine mezze staple. Feel free to go wild and play around with whatever garlic you may have on hand; smoked, green garlic or black.

Add the labneh, garlic, mint leaves and sea salt to a bowl and whip to combine. Divide the mixture between two small serving bowls or one large one and using a spoon create a shallow crater in the middle. Drizzle over the olive oil. Serve chilled with Mini Arabic bread puffs (page 30).

YOU SAY KASHK, I SAY KISHK: FROM AGED BUTTERMILK TO FERMENTED PORRIDGE

From the Levant to the Balkans there is a long list of fermented grain and dried yoghurt products, known under the guises of *kishk*, *kashk*, *kasha*, *kurut* and more. But despite their similar names it is a mistake to loop them all together as one and the same thing, when in fact, they are diverse and very different.

The earliest recorded appearance of the root word kashk is in its Armenian form *k'ashken* around the fifth or sixth century. It likely came from a Persian term meaning 'preparation from barley' pointing to a porridge-like history. Fermenting grain with water or milk-products for porridge has been taking place since the dawn of the agricultural revolution. In fact, porridge and gruel were more of a staple than bread, due to the ease of preparation, and every culture has developed its own version of this nourishing food.

The term has diffused across the region to encompass varying pronunciations and preparations. The modern kashk of Iran, for example, is no longer barley-based but an aged buttermilk, kept in liquid form or dried and reconstituted. The same product is known as *qurut* in most of the central Asian countries, where there is also a darker version (black kashk) called *qarehqurut* or *ghare ghoroot*. On the other hand in Jordan, a dried yoghurt product essential to the national dish of *mansaf* is called jameed. This is a yoghurt that has been heavily salted, strained and dried until hard. It's essentially labneh malboudeh (page 98) on steroids. I think of jameed as the desert's pecorino since, although it's traditionally rehydrated into liquid, I prefer it in a pepper shaker and add it wherever I need a heady dose of umami.

We start departing from aged curdled milk products to feast upon fermented porridges and gruel with Greek/Turkish *tarhana*, a fermented or sour 'pasta' (aka *ksinohondros* and similar to medieval England's frumenty) made either with semolina or cracked wheat and yoghurt and then shaped into pellets and dried, at which point

it may also be ground to a fine powder. This ground tarhana, while linguistically different, is the closest relative to the kishk of my childhood (unlike kashk, which isn't).

The kishk I prize is at the end of its processing a fine, snow-white powder. As a child, it's what I grew up savouring in the mountains of Lebanon, and as an adult it's what I smuggle with me on my travels.

Levantine kishk (that is, from Syria, Lebanon and Palestine) is made by fermenting burghul wheat with yoghurt or water, kneading the mixture once or twice a day over 4–7 days until fermentation is complete. At this point, it can be eaten raw, or green (page 104), rolled into balls, left plain or seasoned with spices and herbs and preserved in olive oil (page 105). Alternatively, the mixture is spread onto clean muslin (cheesecloth) and sun-dried for anything from 7 to 9 days. It is then rubbed between the hands to reduce it to a powder and then returned to the sun one last time to remove any lurking humidity. Finally, this kishk flour is put into cotton bags, as my grandmother used to do, or airtight containers, and stored in a dry place, as part of the winter's provision.

Its processing serves a twofold purpose. The beneficial Lactobacillus in the yoghurt goes to work on the starches and sugars in the burghul, creating lactic acid (a preservative), which helps break down the grain's tough structure, making it easier to digest, while also extending the shelf-life of yoghurt.

Kishk is earthy, creamy with tangy undertones and a mouthful of umami, which makes it an acquired taste if made uber-authentic. Most typically, prepared as a thick savoury porridge it's enjoyed for breakfast. In Levantine countries, it's also made into a paste and used as a topping for flatbreads, a filling for turnovers, or as a salad or dip in its 'green' form (i.e. not dried). I love to use kishk flour to thicken soups or gravies or to add umami to popcorn (page 73), and for fermented béchamel aka kishkamel (page 205).

POOR MAN'S GREEN KISHK

(POOR GARY)

makes   30–36 balls or
         3 x 500 ml (17 fl oz/
         2 cups) jars (serves
         8 as part of a multi-
         course menu)
prep   10 minutes, plus
         fermenting time

700 g (1 lb 9 oz) very fine
    burghul, rinsed and drained
2–3 teaspoons flaky sea salt,
    plus extra to taste
1–2 tablespoons nigella seeds
1–2 tablespoons caraway
    seeds
1–2 tablespoons Aleppo
    pepper flakes or dried
    chilli flakes
about 750 ml (25½ fl oz/
    3 cups) olive oil

This vegan version of kishk is commonly called *kishk el foqara* and while literally meaning 'the kishk of the poor' in Arabic, it may have developed as a corruption of the Persian kashkul, meaning 'beggar's bowl'. But, how could something immersed in so much olive oil be 'of the poor'? That's because this too can be dried like the dairy-version overleaf to create kishk flour, negating the need for all of that olive oil. This fermented 'gary' can be used as a substitute for labneh. Using wholewheat burghul will help the mixture ferment better than white burghul, but I prefer the white purely for colour. This 'gary' takes up to two weeks to ferment.

Add the burghul, salt and 1 litre (34 fl oz/4 cups) lukewarm water to a large non-metallic mixing bowl. Use your hands to knead. Cover with a dark tea towel and leave in a dry, dark place for the mixture to begin fermenting. During the first 3 days, when the day is at its hottest, place the bowl outdoors, still wrapped in the tea towel, and leave in direct sunlight. (This helps to accelerate the fermentation process.) Knead the mixture once every day for these first 3 days. Continue kneading the mixture every second day for the remainder of the time. The fermentation process should take 12–14 days. You are after a subtle fermentation smell; it should not be rancid. Once the mixture has fermented, knead it once more (the mixture should be smooth), pinch a little off and mould to golf ball size. If it needs to be softer or a just little more cohesive, blitz in a food process or for a few pulses. Taste and adjust the salt accordingly.

To make the balls, roll the mixture into roughly 20 g (¾ oz) balls. You should get roughly 30–36 balls. Combine the spices on a plate and roll the balls in the spice mixture, then pack them into sterilised jars. Divide the oil between jars and make sure the balls are completely covered. Place the lids on the jars but don't secure them, and leave in the fridge overnight. The next day, give the jars a gentle shake to allow any gas to escape, then seal and store in a cool, dark place for at least 1 week before serving. Store in the fridge once opened for up to 6 months.

For drying process, see Green kishk overleaf.

GREEN KISHK

makes 625 g (1 lb 6 oz),
yielding 27–30 balls
prep 5 minutes, plus
fermenting time

175 g (6 oz) very fine burghul
475 g (1 lb 1 oz) full-fat Greek
yoghurt (FAGE®), plus extra
as needed
1 teaspoon flaky sea salt
300 ml (10 fl oz/1¼ cups)
olive oil (optional)

Green, or *akhdar* in Arabic, is indicative here of freshness or rawness rather than colour. Once mixed, the ingredients are left to develop in flavour over 3 days. I usually prepare a large batch, divide it into portions and freeze it or preserve it as per below. If taking it out of the freezer, once thawed, freshen it with a spoonful of yoghurt, then add your fresh ingredients.

You need to make sure you're using the finest grade of burghul, which can be found at Middle Eastern grocers and online. For a gluten-free version, replace the burghul with quinoa or buckwheat. Green kishk can be served as is on the table, or used as a filling for pizzettes (page 112).

In a large non-metallic bowl, combine the burghul and 300 g (10½ oz) of the yoghurt. Cover with a clean tea towel and leave in a cool place or a fridge overnight or for at least 24 hours.

The burghul will now have absorbed all the moisture from the yoghurt. Stir in the remaining yoghurt and knead well, then cover and return to the fridge. Leave for 3–5 days, removing and kneading the mixture every 12 hours. If it feels too dry, add a bit more yoghurt. You're after a light fermentation smell that's just slightly sour and the consistency of soft labneh.

If storing as balls, roll into about 20 g (¾ oz) balls (you should get roughly 27–30 balls), gently pack into a sterilised jar and pour over the olive oil, making sure the kishk balls are immersed in oil. Place the lid on but don't secure. Leave overnight in a cool place. The next day, give the jar a gentle shake to allow any gas to escape, then seal and store in a cool, dark place for up to 3 months. Store in the fridge once opened.

If making kishk flour, once the kishk (either this milk-based version or the vegan mixture on page 102) has reached peak fermentation, spread it onto a clean tea towel in one flat layer and cover it with muslin (cheesecloth), then leave to air-dry in the sun for at least 5–7 days. When very dry, crumble into a fine powder and use in recipes such as the Kishkeeya soup (page 191), Pizzettes (page 112) and Kishkamel moussaka (page 205).

GREEN KISHK MUTABAL

makes   about 1 x 475 ml
        (16 fl oz) jar
prep   10 minutes,
        plus overnight
        fermenting time

175–200 g (6–7 oz) Green
  kishk (opposite) or
  Poor man's green
  kishk (page 102)
handful fresh spiked za'atar
  leaves, or handful dried
  thyme or oregano sprigs
1–2 tablespoons Aleppo
  pepper flakes or dried
  chilli flakes
70 g (2½ oz/⅓ cup) pitted
  and chopped green olives
80 g (2¾ oz/⅔ cup)
  walnuts, finely chopped
175–200 ml (6–7 fl oz)
  olive oil

This is delicious stuffed in artichokes like in the recipe on page 109. It's equally good as a multi-purpose dip that you can serve at a moment's notice with Arabic bread, as stuffing for pastries (pages 112 and 116), or alongside potatoes and green salads. Note: the recipe calls for Green kishk or Poor man's green kishk once either have undergone peak fermentation.

Combine the kishk with all the ingredients except the oil and spoon into a sterilised jar. Pour over the oil, making sure to cover the surface of the kishk. Place the lid on the jar but don't secure. Leave in the fridge overnight.

The next day, give the jar a gentle shake to allow any gas to escape. Eat immediately or store in a cool, dark place for up to 3 months. Store in the fridge for one month once opened.

ARTICHOKE

STUFFED WITH GREEN KISHK MUTABAL

serves 6-8 as part of
        a multi-course
        menu
prep   45 minutes

2-3 whole globe artichokes
squeeze lemon juice
½ quantity Green kishk
  mutabal (page 105), or
  more to taste
olive oil (optional)
flaky sea salt

Traditionally, we serve whole artichokes, when in season, at any *aazeeme* or gathering, though no one ever wants to waver from the typical garlic, lemon and olive oil dressing for dipping the leaves into. Here's a much-needed taste of fresh fare, which has gained a following with fellow Lebanese friends, too. A great appetiser to make ahead of time. Stored in the fridge it will last up to 2–3 days. Bring to room temperature or slightly heat through before serving.

Wash and then clip the thorny edges of the artichokes with kitchen shears. Transfer the artichokes to a large pan, fill with water and add a handful of salt and a squeeze of lemon juice. Cover and bring to a boil over high heat, reduce the heat and simmer for 30-45 minutes. Check them halfway through cooking – the artichoke leaves should come away at a gentle tug but the artichokes should still hold their shape.

Place 1-2 heaped spoonfuls of green kishk mutabal into a shallow serving bowl. Place the artichokes into the bowl, opening each up gently like a flower, and using a spoon to stuff them with the kishk then sprinkle with salt to season. Whisk 2-3 tablespoons oil into the remaining tapenade to help loosen it, if needed, and drizzle over the stuffed artichokes. Tear away at the artichoke and use the leaves for dipping, using your teeth to scoop the delicious flesh from the base.

SFIHA STARS

WITH AUBERGINE, WALNUT & POMEGRANATE

makes   about 30–35 (serves
         6–8 as part of a
         multi-course menu)
prep   20 minutes, plus
         preparing and
         resting the dough
cook   10 minutes

1 x quantity Savoury pastry
   dough (opposite)
olive oil, to grease
flour, to dust

for the filling:
1 tablespoon olive oil
1 aubergine (eggplant),
   charred, peeled and
   drained (page 26),
   chopped, or 125 g (4 oz)
   cooked aubergine, very
   finely chopped (excess
   juices drained)
50 g (1¾ oz/½ cup) walnuts,
   chopped
1 garlic clove, finely minced
½ teaspoon Aleppo pepper
   flakes or dried chilli flakes
¼ teaspoon seven spices
   (page 33)
½ teaspoon dried mint
3 tablespoons pomegranate
   molasses
flaky sea salt and freshly
   ground black pepper

Sfiha are traditional meat pies that are left open in order to adjust the seasoning; whether by adding a squeeze of lemon or a dollop of labneh. I make this mock-meat version during Lent. See photo on page 162–163.

Preheat the oven to 200°C/400°F/Gas 6 and lightly grease a baking sheet with oil.

Add the strained and chopped aubergine flesh to a mixing bowl with the walnuts, garlic, spices, mint and pomegranate molasses. Mix well and season with salt and pepper to taste.

On a well-floured work surface, roll the dough out into a large round about 2 mm thick. If necessary, divide it in half and roll it out and stamp it in two stages. For best results, you may find it helps to flip the dough a few times between rolling and sprinkling more flour. Using a 7 cm (3 in) pastry cutter, or cup, cut out 30–35 rounds. Re-roll any pastry scraps and cut out the remaining dough.

To fill, place 1 teaspoon of the stuffing in the centre of each circle. Using thumb and index finger, pinch the edges of the dough, going around the circumference 5 times, to reach a star shape. Pinch together tightly into the shape of a star, and keep pinching until you see no crease (you want to eliminate the crease between the two layers of dough that you are bringing together at each of the five points, to ensure they stay sealed during cooking. Otherwise, the dough will open up to a pizette.

Place the sfiha on the prepared sheet and bake for 7–10 minutes, or until golden and crisp at the edges. Serve hot or at room temperature.

Also try: The sfiha stars can be shaped and frozen in an airtight container for up to 8 weeks. Cook them from frozen as per above, increasing the cooking time by 2–3 minutes. You can also freeze the pastries once baked. To heat, pop them straight into an oven preheated to 200°C/400°F/Gas 6 for 10 minutes, or until heated through.

SAVOURY PASTRY DOUGH

makes enough dough for
30–35 fatayer
prep 10 minutes,
plus 1 hour
for rising

150 g (5½ oz/1 cup) plain
(all-purpose) flour, plus
extra for dusting
½ teaspoon flaky sea salt
1 teaspoon caster
(superfine) sugar
4 tablespoons olive oil, plus
extra for greasing
6 tablespoons full-fat milk
½ teaspoon dried
active yeast

Here is a basic pastry dough recipe used for the array of savoury pastries or *fatayer* that grace any Middle Eastern dinner party, buffet or mezze.

Sift the flour, salt and sugar into a mound on a clean work surface and create a well in the middle. Pour the oil into the centre of the well and, using your hands, start incorporating the flour until fully combined.

Heat the milk in a saucepan until tepid, then pour it into a small bowl. Sprinkle over the yeast and mix thoroughly. Add the yeast mixture to the flour and oil mixture and knead for about 5 minutes, dusting the work surface with flour as necessary, or until smooth and elastic and a ball has formed.

Place the dough into a large bowl greased with a little oil, and score the top with a knife to loosen the surface tension. Cover with a damp, clean tea towel and place in a warm, draught-free place for about 1 hour until doubled in size. Use as required in the recipes opposite and on pages 115 and 116.

SPICED KISHK PIZZETTES

makes   32–40 (serves
        8–12 as part of
        a multi-course
        menu)
prep   25 minutes,
        plus preparing
        and resting
        the dough
cook   25 minutes

1 x quantity Arabic bread
   dough (page 30)

for the topping:
7 tablespoons kishk flour
   (page 107) or crumbled firm
   labneh (page 28) or feta
½ teaspoon flaky sea salt
3 garlic cloves,
   finely chopped
2 teaspoons dried mint
2 teaspoons smoked paprika
2 teaspoons Aleppo pepper
   flakes or dried chilli flakes
½ teaspoon ground turmeric
2 tablespoons olive oil, plus
   extra for brushing
175–200 g (6–7 oz) sujuk,
   Bacon basturma (page 95)
   or chorizo, diced
3–4 heirloom tomatoes, very
   thinly sliced, or 2 handfuls
   cherry tomatoes

These little pizzettes are inspired by my aunt Janane. Her table always has little pizzettes with ham and black olives, which I loved devouring. *Sujuk* is a heavily-spiced, semi-dry sausage. Feel free to substitute the sujuk for chorizo or Bacon basturma (page 95).

Make the pastry dough according to the recipe on page 111.

In a mixing bowl, add all the ingredients for the filling and combine with 250 ml (8½ fl oz/1 cup) hot water. Stir well. The texture should be spreadable but not very wet.

Preheat the oven to 200°C/400°F/Gas 6 and grease baking sheet with oil.

Divide the dough into 4 balls. Take one dough ball and roll it out to about ½ cm (¼ in) thick and then, using a ramekin, or a 7 cm (3 in) pastry cutter, cut out about 8 rounds. Transfer to a baking sheet and spread about ½ teaspoon of the kishk mixture on top of each round and top with a tomato slice. Bake in the oven for about 7 minutes, or until the edges of the pizzettes are golden and crispy. Repeat with the remaining 3 balls. Serve with a selection of mezze dishes, if you like.

Also try: You can also freeze the pizzettes baked or unbaked for up to 8 weeks in an airtight container. To heat, pop them straight into an oven preheated to 200°C/400°F/Gas 6 for 10 minutes, or until heated through.

PRAWN CRESCENTS

makes	about 30–35 (serves 6–8 as part of a multi-course menu)
prep	20 minutes, plus preparing and resting the dough
cook	20 minutes

1 x quantity Savoury pastry
  dough (page 111)

for the filling:
2 tablespoons olive oil
½ onion (about 75 g/½ oz),
  very finely chopped
150 g (5½ oz) raw prawns
  (shrimp), finely chopped
2–3 tablespoons chopped
  coriander (cilantro)
2 tablespoons Smoked
  tomato hot sauce (page 76)
  or hot sauce
2 tablespoons soy sauce
4 garlic cloves, very finely
  chopped
1 tablespoon ground sumac
zest of 1 lime or small lemon
small handful green olives,
  pitted and chopped
rapeseed oil, for deep-frying
flaky sea salt and freshly
  ground black pepper

Traditionally, the filling for the crescents is either cheese or meat but I thought I'd be a little more creative and use a prawn one. It's certainly been a winner with my crowd. Serve with Fenugreek relish (page 79). The crescents can be shaped and frozen in an airtight container for up to 2 months. Cook them from frozen, increasing the cooking time by 2–3 minutes.

Place a small non-stick pan over medium heat, add the olive oil and sauté the onion for 3–4 minutes, stirring often, until soft and translucent. Add the prawns, cook through for a further 1–2 minutes until pink in colour, then add the coriander, smoked tomato hot sauce, soy sauce, garlic, sumac, lime zest and olives. Season to taste and add a little more hot sauce if you feel you and your guests can tolerate it. The stuffing needs to be sharp to cut through the dough. Mix well to combine and set aside.

Flour a working surface and divide the dough into two. Keep one portion covered in a damp tea towel to keep it moist. Working with the other portion, roll it out into a large circle, about 2 mm thick. You may find it helps to flip the dough a few times during the rolling stage, dusting with flour as needed. Using a pastry cutter, or cup, cut out rounds of about 7 cm (3 in) in diameter. Re-roll any pastry scraps and cut out the remaining dough. You should end up with about 30–35 rounds.

To fill, place about 1 heaped teaspoon of the prawn mixture just off centre of each circle, fold the dough over and, using your thumb and index finger, seal the edges together to create a half-moon shape. Return to the end that is nearest from you, and begin pleating the sealed edge with your fingers by making tight, overlapping diagonal folds and repeat. You will have a little excess dough by the end of the 'braiding', twist this off, and tuck the edge into the dough, sealing tightly.

To deep-fry the crescents, fill a large saucepan (or deep fryer) one-third with oil and place over high heat until the oil reaches 180°C/350°F on a thermometer. Alternatively, test the temperature by carefully dipping in the edge of a crescent parcel with a slotted spoon – if the oil sizzles, it's ready. Deep-fry the crescents, in batches to avoid overcrowding the pan, until light golden. They should take about 2 minutes per side. Don't leave them unattended, as they can quickly burn. Using a slotted spoon, transfer the crescents to a paper-towel-lined plate. Leave to cool slightly and serve.

BEETROOT, LABNEH & ZA'ATAR FATAYER KAYAKS

makes 30–35 (serves 4–8 as part of a multi-course menu)
prep 20 minutes, plus preparing and resting the dough
cook 10 minutes

1 x quantity Savoury pastry dough (page 111)
olive oil, to grease
flour, for dusting

for the filling:
1 cooked beetroot (beet) (about 100 g/3½ oz), peeled and finely chopped
120 g (4½ oz) firm labneh (page 28) or feta, crumbled
1–2 heaped tablespoons fresh or dried za'atar
zest of ¼ grapefruit
2 tablespoons olive oil
flaky sea salt and freshly ground black pepper

Fatayer is the generic name for pastries encompassing all shapes: stars (page 110), pizzettes (page 112) or crescents (page 115). The filling speaks for itself but if I may add my two cents: simply scrumptioulescent! You can substitute the labneh with Green kishk mutabal (page 105).

Preheat the oven to 200°C/400°F/Gas 6 and generously grease a baking sheet with oil.

To make the filling, combine the beetroot, labneh, za'atar, grapefruit zest and oil in a mixing bowl and season with salt and pepper to taste.

Flour a working surface and divide the dough into two. Keep one portion covered in a damp tea towel to keep it moist. Working with the other portion, roll it out into a large circle, about 2 mm thick. You may find it helps to flip the dough a few times during the rolling stage, dusting with flour as needed. Using a 7 cm (3 in) pastry cutter, or cup, cut out 30–35 rounds. Re-roll any pastry scraps and cut out the remaining dough.

To fill, place 1 teaspoon of the mixture in the centre of each circle. Using thumb and index finger, pinch the opposing edges of the dough to form a boat shape. Pinch together tightly, and thin out gently until you see no crease – you want to eliminate the crease between the two layers of dough that you are bringing together at the opposing points, to ensure they stay sealed during cooking. Otherwise, the dough will open up to a pizette.

Place the 'kayaks' on the prepared sheet and bake for 7–10 minutes, or until golden and crisp at the edges. Serve hot or at room temperature.

Also try: Freeze the cooked or uncooked fatayer kayaks in an airtight container for up to 8 weeks. They can be baked from frozen in an oven preheated to 200°C/400°F/Gas 6 for 10–15 minutes, or until heated through.

NOURA'S DECEPTIVE VINE LEAVES

STUFFED WITH TABBOULEH & ARABIC COFFEE

makes   about 50, serves
         8-10 as part of
         a multi-course
         menu
prep   1 hour
cook   2-3 hours

500 g (1 lb 2 oz/50-60)
  vine leaves (from a jar or
  vacuum-packed), rinsed
1 large tomato, thinly sliced
1 onion, thinly sliced
1 teaspoon fine sea salt
1 lemon, thinly sliced
full-fat Greek yoghurt,
  to serve

for the filling:
60 ml (2 fl oz/¼ cup)
  olive oil
1 onion, finely chopped
6 garlic cloves, 3 finely
  chopped and 3 smashed
75 g (2¾ oz) parsley,
  finely chopped
handful mint leaves,
  finely chopped
½ red (bell) pepper,
  finely chopped
3 tomatoes, finely chopped
1 teaspoon tomato paste
5 tablespoons pomegranate
  molasses
3 heaped tablespoons
  Arabic coffee (page 50)
  (optional)
½ teaspoon Aleppo pepper
  flakes or dried chilli flakes
pinch of ground allspice
250 g (9 oz/¾ cup) short-
  grain rice
flaky sea salt and freshly
  ground black pepper

Noura, our gardener's wife, shared this lovely recipe with me. Most vegetarian stuffings are essentially a mixture of leftover tabbouleh mixed with rice or burghul. I love this version, which incorporates coffee. *Yalangi* from Turkish *yalancı* means 'liar' as the filling deceptively omits meat. According to Noura (who looked at me like a deer in headlights when I mentioned proportions), the amount below would likely be the smallest pot of vine leaves ever made in the Middle East. You can scale down the recipe, but you'll need to find a small heavy-based pan to keep the parcels bundled up and compact.

First, prepare the vine leaves. Remove the vine leaves from the packaging or brine and carefully separate the leaves, one by one, transferring them to the bowl of warm water. Leave to soak for about 10 minutes. Change the water and leave to soak for a further 10 minutes. Drain, then rinse under cold water. Shake off the excess water and transfer the leaves to a chopping board. Cut the hard stems out and set aside.

Place a small frying pan over medium heat, add the oil and the chopped onion, and fry for 10 minutes until slightly golden. Add the finely chopped garlic and cook for a further minute. Transfer to a large mixing bowl with the remaining oil, and parsley, mint, red pepper, chopped tomatoes, tomato paste, pomegranate molasses, coffee (if using), chilli flakes, allspice and rice. Season with salt and pepper and mix well to combine.

Arrange the tomato slices in one layer in a deep, heavy-based saucepan. Top with the onion slices and sprinkle with fine salt.

On a chopping board, working with one at a time, place a vine leaf with the shiny side down and the wide base of the leaf facing you. (You may need to layer up with another vine leaf if any have holes in them.) Place 1 teaspoon of the filling about 1 cm (½ in) up from the base. Roll the leaf over the filling and fold in the sides to form a tight cylindrical shape, finishing with the seam-side down. Repeat with the remaining vine leaves and stuffing. Use kitchen string to bundle the parcels up in groups of five or ten, this will keep the stuffing from escaping during cooking. Arrange the parcels over the tomato and onion layer; make sure they sit snugly inside the pan. Drop in the smashed garlic and lemon slices. Weigh the parcels down using an inverted heatproof plate. Pour in enough salted water for the level to come up to about 5 cm (2 in) above the plate. Place a tight-fitting lid on the pan, and bring to the boil over a medium heat. Reduce the heat to low and simmer gently for 1½-2 hours or until the vine leaves are meltingly smooth and the surrounding liquid has thickened. During this time, check the water level and top up if the vine leaves appear dry.

Remove the pan from the heat and leave to rest for 10–15 minutes. Remove the kitchen string around the parcels, and serve warm or at room temperature with yoghurt.

RAW BEETROOT TARTARE KNUCKLES

WITH SHALLOT VINAIGRETTE

serves 4-6 as part of
a multi-course
menu
prep 10 minutes

for the mint vinaigrette:
2 shallots, roughly chopped
3.5 cm (1½ in) piece ginger,
 peeled and roughly
 chopped
handful mint leaves
60 ml (2 fl oz/¼ cup) cider
 vinegar
100 ml (3½ fl oz) olive oil
flaky sea salt

160 g (5½ oz) very fine
 burghul, rinsed and drained
360 g (12½ oz) candy or
 regular beetroot (beets),
 peeled and grated
freshly grated nutmeg
½ teaspoon fine sea salt
⅛ teaspoon ground cloves
¼ teaspoon ground
 cinnamon
¼ teaspoon ground allspice
½ teaspoon ground cumin
40 g (1½ oz/⅓ cup) walnuts,
 toasted and roughly
 chopped

I have not come across any Middle Easterner that does not adore kebbeh. The Levantine pièce de résistance, spiced burghul (or rice or semolina) is kneaded with minced meat, pulses or grated vegetables, to create a paste that is moulded into a variety of shapes and cooked in different ways. Some other examples I've shared in this book are the Golden rice kebbeh teardrops (page 122) and Loquat kebbeh (page 214).

Make the vinaigrette. In small food processor, add the shallots, ginger, mint, vinegar and oil and blitz. Adjust acidity levels and oil and pulse once more, taste, season with salt and set aside.

Place the burghul in a bowl with the salt along with 100 ml (3½ fl oz/ ½ cup) just-boiled water, and leave to sit for 5 minutes. Add the beetroot and spices. Mix well, fluff with a fork, then transfer to a food processor and blitz for 2-3 minutes or until the mixture feels cohesive.

Using heavy pressure of your palms (have a plate placed beneath), create 12 mostly even spiked 'knuckle' shapes, and reuse any leftover mixture. Serve with the vinaigrette drizzled over and the walnuts sprinkled atop.

GOLDEN RICE KEBBEH TEARDROPS

WITH DUCK & ORANGE BLOSSOM

makes	30–35 teardrops serves 8 as part of a multi-course menu
prep	20 minutes
cook	40 minutes

pinch of saffron threads
  or ½ teaspoon ground
  turmeric
2 tablespoons fine sea salt
450 g (1 lb/2 cups) jasmine
  or short-grain rice
zest of 1 orange
olive oil, for brushing
Smoked tomato hot sauce
  (page 76) or hot sauce,
  to serve

for the filling:
2 tablespoons olive oil
1 onion, finely chopped
275 g (9½ oz) minced
  (ground) duck, venison,
  turkey or lamb
½ teaspoon ground
  cinnamon
½ tablespoon seven spices
  (page 33)
½ teaspoon ground
  black pepper
½ teaspoon ground
  white pepper
1 tablespoon dried marjoram
1 tablespoon dried sage
50 g (1¾ oz/⅓ cup)
  almonds, toasted and
  finely chopped
2 tablespoons orange
  blossom water
handful sultanas (optional)
flaky sea salt

This recipe is for an Iraqi kebbeh, known as *kebbet timman* (rice kebbeh). The use of rice rather than burghul also makes this kebbeh gluten free. Traditionally, the teardrops are fried but I like them baked. They are excellent served with any of the whipped hummus recipes (pages 174 and 177–180) or the Cucumber and mint yoghurt (page 81).

Place a large saucepan over medium-high heat and pour in 2 litres (68 fl oz/8 cups) water. Add the saffron and salt, and bring to a boil. Once the water is boiling, add in the rice, stir and cook, uncovered, for 15–20 minutes, checking the texture of the rice halfway through the cooking time. You're after fully cooked grain, not one that is crumbly or mushy. When the rice is cooked, strain well immediately, then transfer back to the pan and set aside to cool.

Meanwhile, prepare the filling. Heat the oil in heavy-based saucepan and cook the onion over medium heat for 3–4 minutes, stirring often. Stir in the meat, spices and herbs and cook for a few more minutes, using a wooden spoon to break down the meat, until cooked through. Season to taste with salt and then add the almonds, orange blossom water, and sultanas if using. Stir well, taste and adjust the seasoning, then set aside and allow to cool briefly.

Preheat the oven to 200°C/400°F/Gas 6. Line a baking tray with baking (parchment) paper.

Return to the rice, which should have cooled by now. Add the orange zest and squeeze the rice into a paste. You can use a food processor though I prefer using my hands. This should take 3–4 minutes. Taste and adjust seasoning, then divide the mixture into roughly 30–35 (20–25 g/¾–1 oz) balls and set on a tray.

Fill a small bowl with iced water. Working with each ball at a time and dipping your fingers in the water if needed, hollow-out the centre using your thumb, then fill each well with about a teaspoon of the filling. Using your thumb, middle finger and index finger, seal the top into a fine point, making sure to gently flatten the bottom of the ball, so that it can stand upright. Transfer to the prepared tray. Continue moulding the balls until done.

Brush the teardrops with oil and bake in the oven for about 45 minutes, or until golden and crisp. Serve immediately with smoked tomato hot sauce for dipping.

4

UNFASTEN THE APPETITE

SMALL PLATES AND ADDITIONAL DISHES

BEFORE WHAT IS TO COME

Muqabilat can be loosely translated to mean 'things before what is to come'. Muqabilat therefore is the Arabic equivalent for appetiser. Although 'mezze' is used interchangeably for the same meaning, there lies a deep distinction.

While many of the muqabilat dishes are without a doubt the same dishes you'd see on a mezze spread, and often served in the same quantity and order, the concept of mezze is that it is a meal made up of a procession of small dishes or nibbles without a 'main', attention-grabbing, substantial dish. There is no follow-up meal, but dishes that could fall into the 'main' category can be served in small 'mezze' portions. Mezze is also essentially the reserve of dining establishments. Muqabilat are part of a typical meal or feast set in a Middle Eastern home, and devised around a substantial or show-stopping main (see chapter 5). While these dishes grace the table as appetisers, they also remain part of the meal till the end, which is why muqabilat can also be referred to as *aklat idafeeya*, or 'additional dishes' as they can be served before the main and along with the main, in the same instance.

Muqabilat dishes are varied. Usually the cold selections decorate the sofra first, such as the cooked vegetable salads, bawarid and zeytiyat (see 'A dish best served cold', page 136) and the warmer ones follow when everyone sits at the table. Breaking of bread begins and the appetite is unfastened.

'MEFTEH EL BATEN LE'ME'

'THE KEY TO AN APPETITE IS IN THE FIRST BITE'

KUKU

WITH GREEN STALKS AND HERBS

serves   4–6 as part of
         a multi-course
         menu
prep   20 minutes
cook   20 minutes

4 tablespoons olive oil
1 leek, thinly sliced
200 g (7 oz) mixed soft
    green stalks and/or herbs
    (equal parts beetroot/
    beets, carrots, radishes
    and kohlrabi and choice of
    soft herbs), finely chopped
3 garlic cloves, finely
    chopped
½ teaspoon ground turmeric
½ teaspoon ground
    coriander
½ teaspoon ground ginger
¼ teaspoon ground
    cinnamon
flaky sea salt
8–10 eggs, beaten

This dish is inspired by the Arab *eggah* and Persian herb frittata
known as *kuku sabzi*. The original egg omelette dish uses a mixture
of herbs, but this recipe uses things you might otherwise throw away.
Here I've opted for the stalks from beetroot, carrots, radishes and
kohlrabi. You can adapt it to your taste, using any leftover edible stalks
and herbs you have on hand, or even the leftover innards from any of
the stuffed dishes on pages 208–213. If you want a meatier option you
can add some Bacon basturma (page 95) or chorizo and mix through
a few tablespoons of yoghurt to cut through the richness.

Preheat your grill (broiler) to high.

Place a large ovenproof pan (one that will fit under the grill) over medium
heat, then add 2 tablespoons of the oil and leave to heat for about
30 seconds. Add the leek and sauté for a minute, stirring often. Add in
the stalks and/or herbs, and cook for about 5 minutes, stirring often
until the stalks have wilted. Stir in the garlic and spices and season with
salt. Mix well. Taste and adjust the seasoning to taste. Use a spatula to
spread the greens evenly across the bottom of the pan, drizzle over the
remaining oil, then pour over the eggs. Tilt the pan gently to help spread
the eggs evenly and then leave to cook for 3–4 minutes, or until bubbles
gently begin to develop on the top of the kuku.

Finish cooking the kuku under the grill for 3–4 minutes, or until the edges
turn a lovely golden brown. Alternatively, finish cooking the kuku on the
stovetop by reducing the heat to low, covering it with a lid and cooking
until just done (about 3–4 minutes).

Remove from heat and leave to cool for 5 minutes. Slice up and serve
warm or at room temperature with bread.

SULTAN'S POACHED EGGS

WITH BRAISED RAINBOW CHARD YOGHURT, SWEET POTATO FRITTERS & BASTURMA BUTTER

serves   6
prep   20 minutes
cook   30-40 minutes

for the potato fritters:
250 g (9 oz) sweet potato,
    peeled and coarsely grated
1 tablespoon flaky sea salt
4 tablespoons plain (all-
    purpose) flour
45 ml (1½ fl oz) olive oil

for the chard yoghurt:
115 g (4 oz) rainbow or
    regular Swiss chard, or
    baby spinach
2-3 garlic cloves, very
    finely chopped
400 g (14 oz/scant 1⅔ cups)
    full-fat Greek yoghurt, at
    room temperature
100 g (3½ oz/⅔ cup)
    crumbled feta
flaky sea salt

75-90 g (2¾-3 oz) Aged
    butter (page 29) or
    clarified butter or
    2 tablespoons olive oil
60-75 g (2-2¾ oz) Bacon
    basturma (page 97) or
    chorizo, roughly chopped
12 freshest eggs, at room
    temperature
olive oil, for shallow frying

to serve:
1 tablespoon Aleppo pepper
    flakes or dried chilli flakes
1 tablespoon ground sumac
handful tarragon,
    roughly chopped

The recipe title might be a mouthful, but it's the most luxurious mouthful you'll come to have; Ottoman Palace food at its finest. *Çılbır*, pronounced 'chillber' does not appear to have a common meaning. Always hungry to get to the root of every word, I finally came across a reading that suggested it is a middle Mongolian loan word from *cilbure*, which translates as 'leather reins'. Perhaps, the name applied either because the egg whites tend to get stringy when poached or because a punctured yolk spilling into the yoghurt could resemble reins. Whichever the case, one bite of this and you're going to be led back for more.

For a vegetarian take, substitute the basturma with roughly chopped walnuts. If you're short on time, you can fry the eggs, omit the sweet potato hash and serve it simply with Griddled flatbread (page 36).

Place the grated sweet potato in a bowl with the salt. Mix together well and set aside.

Meanwhile, heat the Aged butter or olive oil for the braised chard in a saucepan over medium-low heat, add the chard and season with a pinch of salt, then sauté, stirring often, until wilted. Strain, leaving a little of the water from the chard in the pan, and return to the heat, then add the garlic. Cook for 30-60 seconds, then remove from the heat. Pour over the yoghurt and crumbled feta, and mix well to combine. Cover and set aside somewhere warm.

As the water is coming to a simmer, return to the sweet potatoes and strain them very well of any excess liquid. Toss in the flour.

Add enough olive oil to a pan so that it's about 3.5 cm (1 in) deep, and heat until sizzling. To make the fritters, use your hands to mould them into small patties, then add to the pan, five at a time, being careful not to break them, and cook for 4-5 minutes on each side until golden brown. Reduce the heat to prevent them burning. Transfer to a paper-towel-lined plate and keep warm. Repeat with the remaining mixture, adding more oil as needed.

Wipe the pan using paper towels and place back over medium heat. Add the butter and basturma. Cook for a few minutes, until the butter has melted and the basturma has slightly browned. Keep warm.

To poach the eggs, bring a large pan of water to a simmer. Line a small ramekin with a square of cling film (plastic wrap), brush lightly with oil and crack an egg into it. Bring the edges of the cling film together and twist using excess cling film to secure. Repeat with the remaining eggs. Lower the pouches carefully into the pan of simmering water and cook for 2-3 minutes. Remove using a slotted spoon and leave to cool enough to handle, then carefully remove the cling film.

To serve, swirl a few dollops of the chard yoghurt in shallow serving bowls. Top with the sweet potato fritter, the egg and then drizzle over the bacon butter. Sprinkle with the chilli flakes, sumac and tarragon, and serve.

ORANGE BLOSSOM CHICKEN BARIDA

serves 8 as part of
        a multi-course
        menu
prep   15 minutes
cook   10 minutes

for the filling:
275 g (9½ oz) cooked and
  shredded chicken
2 celery stalks, finely sliced
½ red onion, finely chopped
2 tablespoons dried
  barberries or currants
handful walnuts,
  finely chopped
1 small cucumber, diced
15–20 black olives, pitted
  and finely chopped
seeds of ½ pomegranate,
  plus extra for sprinkling
8 heaped tablespoons soft
  labneh (page 25)
2 tablespoons mustard
2 tablespoons white
  wine vinegar
splash of orange
  blossom water

1–2 Lebanese flatbreads
olive oil, for greasing

Chicken salad may seem retro, but this one is positively medieval. It's a timely resurrection of a much-loved dish, described as the perfect summertime fare by Ibrahim ibn al-mahdi (poet, musician and cook) who devised this barida dish in the ninth century. The idea behind *bawarid* – cold dishes – is a mixture of meat or vegetables, brought together by a sauce. Timeless. Much like the sandwich... Many believe the sandwich to have been invented in 18th-century England by Lord Sandwich, however, medieval records turn back the clock. At ancient Persian banquets, you'd be served a sort of canapé called *bazmaward* or *awsat*, which was essentially thin flatbread (but not always) filled with roast meat, such as the following baridas, rolled up and sliced into pin-wheels. Today, we call these *aarayes* in parts of the Middle East. Bazmaward make for wonderful snacks or finger food to decorate the table with.

In a mixing bowl, combine all the ingredients for the filling. Serve as a salad or use the filling as a bazmaward (should make 16 pinwheels).

To make the bazmaward, preheat the grill (broiler) to medium-high. Grease a baking tray with a generous amount of oil.

Use a knife to slice through the centres of the flatbreads and spread the filling mixture between the four rounds. Roll up firmly, tucking in the sides, like a burrito. Using a serrated knife, slice into 2.5 cm (1 in) slices. Place on the tray and grill for 5 minutes, or until crisp. Turn them over and repeat on other side. Serve warm.

A DISH BEST SERVED COLD

Serving cooked cold salads is a *leitmotif* of the Middle East and it's not out of cold spite. This ancient practice is obviously going against the whole 'raw' food trend and for good reason. There is something very satiating about vegetables that are cooked, albeit al dente, and where the flavours are encouraged to meld together. This can be best tasted in the glorious cooked tomato salads of North Africa, *matbucha*, and the *allayet* of the Levant (pages 138 and 142). But cooking salads is not where it stops. Serving cooked vegetables cold – and even meat (chicken salad anyone?) – is also an ancient practice, which comes to us documented in Ibn Sayyar's medieval cookbook, *Annals of the Caliphs' Kitchens'*, within a chapter dedicated to bawarid or 'cold dishes', showcasing dishes such as *buran* (page 146). These were also touted for their health benefits, with the physician al-Razi observing that bawarid-style dishes, when made with vinegar or with the juice of sour fruits, have an ability to moderate and cool the temperament.

Then there are the cooked, cold, olive-oil-based dishes, known as *zeytiyat* in the Levant and *zeytinyaglilar* in Turkey, both from the Arabic root word, *zeyt*, meaning oil. The territories of modern-day Syria, Lebanon and Palestine, or Bilad el Sham as they were known, have an abundance of olive orchards and so the oil has become an essential ingredient. Zeytiyat and zeytinyaglilar, are vegetable-focused dishes, which have come to us dictated in part by the Christian religious custom of 40 days of fasting – Lent – as well as from austere, farm-to-table times. They remain some of my favourite dishes, which sustain me through the week and keep my thoughts of meat at bay.

SMOKED MACKEREL & ZHUG BARIDA

serves 8 as part of
a multi-course
menu
prep   10 minutes

for the filling:
275 g (9½ oz) smoked
mackerel, skinned and
shredded
flaky sea salt and freshly
ground black pepper

for the zhug:
4 tablespoons Zhug salsa
(page 77)
zest and juice of ½ lemon

1–2 Lebanese flatbreads
olive oil, for greasing

I love the combination of oily and piquant flavours in this *barida*.
It can be whizzed up in a matter of minutes and is a wonderful
addition to any spread, making for a simple and light lunch when
served with warm flatbreads and crisp salad greens.

Combine the zhug with the lemon juice and zest. Transfer the zhug to a
mixing bowl, add the shredded mackerel and combine well. Pour in half
the lemon juice, taste and adjust the seasoning accordingly. Serve as a
salad or use the filling as a bazmaward (should make 16 pinwheels).

To make the bazmaward, preheat the grill (broiler) to medium-high.
Grease a baking tray with a generous amount of oil.

Use a knife to slice through the centres of the flatbreads and spread the
filling mixture between the four rounds. Roll up firmly, tucking in the sides,
like a burrito. Using a serrated knife, slice into 2.5 cm (1 in) slices. Place on
the tray and grill for 5 minutes, or until crisp. Turn them over and repeat
on other side. Serve warm.

BRAISED TOMATOES

serves   8–10
prep   45 minutes–1 hour,
         including charring
         the vegetables
cook   1 hour 10 minutes

1–2 red (bell) peppers or
  jarred chargrilled peppers,
  drained and chopped
1–2 fresh red chillies
1 kg (2 lb 3 oz) ripe tomatoes
120 ml (4 fl oz/½ cup) olive
  oil, plus extra to drizzle
flaky sea salt
6 garlic cloves, finely
  chopped
1 tablespoon coriander
  seeds, toasted and crushed
1 tablespoon smoked paprika
30 g (1 oz) pine nuts, toasted,
  to serve
1 tablespoon chopped fresh
  coriander (cilantro) leaves,
  to serve

Don't let the basic name of this dish fool you. Hugely popular in North African countries, the dish can be found under several guises across the region: *salata* (salad) *matbucha*, if simply braised on the stovetop, *salata meshweeya*, if the vegetables are grilled (page 142), or *taktouka* if onions are used in place of garlic. There's a simpler version in the Levant where it's known as *allayet banadora*, sometimes with aubergines (eggplants) included.

A true chameleon, this dish is incredibly versatile. Serve it as a dip with pita crisps (page 31) or flatbread, as an accompaniment to fish and meat dishes, as a condiment in sandwiches or as a base to crack eggs into (think shakshouka). Ideally, make the dish when there is a glut of tomatoes as it can be kept in a sterilised jar immersed in olive oil for up to two weeks. Keep it in the fridge for those times you need to add a flavour hit.

If using fresh, char the peppers, chillies and tomatoes according to the instructions on page 22. Deseed the chillies if you prefer. Peel and chop the peppers and tomatoes.

Place a deep, heavy-based frying pan over medium-low heat. Add the oil, peppers and a pinch of salt, and let them sweat until meltingly soft. This should take about 20 minutes. Add the chillies and cook for a further 2 minutes, then stir in the garlic and crushed coriander seeds, and cook for a further 1–2 minutes, stirring often. Add the tomatoes and gently simmer for 30–40 minutes, until softened and intensified in colour. Add the paprika, and salt to taste, and simmer for another 10 minutes or so. Taste and adjust the seasoning if required.

Spoon onto a shallow sharing plate, make a well in the middle and drizzle with extra oil and scatter over the pine nuts. Sprinkle over the chopped coriander and serve at room temperature.

WARM SALAD OF GREENS

WITH OLIVE OIL & ONION TEMPURA

serves 6–8 as part of
        a multi-course
        menu
prep   10 minutes
cook   20 minutes

5 tablespoons olive oil
1 red onion, thinly sliced
3 garlic cloves, finely
  chopped
400 g (7 oz) leafy greens,
  such as wild dandelion,
  baby spinach leaves, kale
  or Swiss chard, any tough
  stalks removed
2 tablespoons ground sumac
½ teaspoon ground allspice
flaky sea salt and freshly
  ground black pepper
1 x quantity Tempura onions
  (page 23)
2–3 tablespoons pine nuts,
  toasted
seeds of ½ pomegranate
lemon wedges, to serve

This braised salad is normally made with dandelion, wild chicory, or other wild foraged greens often available in spring during Lent. The dish falls into the category of *zeytiyat, bawarid* and *aklet sawm* (food for Lent) (page 136). It can be made with any seasonal greens. Fold in a dollop of yoghurt and the salad becomes a modern-day borani (page 148). Add a fried egg, some cooked chickpeas and bread and you've got a satiating lunch sorted.

Place a large pan over medium heat, add 2 tablespoons of the oil and, once sizzling, add the onion and cook for 10–15 minutes, until soft and translucent. Add the garlic and cook, stirring often, until the garlic is aromatic. Add the greens and cook until wilted for 2–3 minutes, stirring often. Season with the sumac, allspice and salt and pepper. Add the remaining oil. Divide the greens between serving plates, place a small mound of onion tempura in the centre and then sprinkle over the pomegranate and pine nuts. Serve with lemon wedges.

GRILLED VEGETABLE SALAD

WITH HALLOUMI & CARROT-TOP CHERMOULA

serves 8–10
prep   20 minutes
cook   30 minutes

for the carrot-top
chermoula (makes enough
to fill 1 x 400 ml
(13½ fl oz/1⅔ cup jar):
300 g (10½ oz) carrot tops
30 g (1 oz) dill,
  including stems
30 g (1 oz) tarragon,
  including stems
30 g (1 oz) ginger, peeled
  and roughly chopped
1 celery stalk, chopped
1 garlic head, peeled
  and smashed
4 cardamom pods, toasted
  and smashed
½ teaspoon cumin
  seeds, toasted
pinch of ground cinnamon
½ preserved lemon,
  seeds removed
3–4 small green chillies
375 ml (12½ fl oz/1½ cups)
  olive oil, plus extra
  if needed

for the salad:
2 aubergines (eggplants),
  sliced lengthways into
  thirds
40 ml (1¼ fl oz) olive oil
1 garlic head, top trimmed
6 cooked artichoke hearts
  (or jarred artichoke hearts),
  rinsed well
1–2 fennel bulbs, sliced
  lengthways in thirds
3 shallots, halved lengthways
2 courgettes (zucchinis),
  sliced lengthways into
  thirds
3 assorted small sweet (bell)
  peppers, sliced lengthways
  in half
3 red chillies, halved
  lengthways
500 g (1 lb 2 oz) halloumi
  cheese, sliced into wedges
flaky sea salt

In North African countries like Libya and Tunisia, *meshweeya* is usually a version of matbucha (page 138) where the vegetables are grilled and then cooked down to a purée. I like offering up this take of meshweeya alongside matbucha, using sliced seasonal vegetables served with a chermoula drizzle; often one using the carrot tops, depending on season. The chermoula recipe makes more than needed for this salad, but keep it in the fridge and used for the Smoked mackerel barida (page 137). It is best made a day or so in advance as this helps to intensify the flavour. You may have some vegetables left over, in which case you can pulverise them to a very rough paste with any remaining drizzle, toss with some cooked couscous or spaghetti and you have tomorrow's lunch sorted.

First, make the chermoula. Place the ingredients in a food processor and pulse for 1–2 minutes to form a paste-like consistency. Season with salt to taste. Add more oil if needed. You can prepare this up to a few days in advance and store it in the fridge.

Preheat the grill (broiler) or barbecue to medium-high. When hot, baste the aubergines all over with 40 ml (1½ fl oz) oil, sprinkle with salt and grill for 5–10 minutes, or until softened and lightly browned all over. Brush with a little of the chermoula during the final 5 minutes of cooking. Repeat with the remaining vegetables, basting with chermoula, until nicely browned at the edges.

Remove the vegetables to a serving plate and grill the halloumi for 5–8 minutes.

Serve with some of the chermoula.

FROM MAGHMOUR & BORONIA TO MUSAQA'A

serves   8 as part of
          a multi-course
          menu
prep   30 minutes
cook   1 hour

500 g (1 lb 2 oz) aubergines
    (eggplants) (about 2 large)
1 red (bell) pepper, ideally
    romano
500 g (1 lb 2 oz) tomatoes
60 ml (2 fl oz/¼ cup) olive
    oil
1 large onion, thinly sliced
5 garlic cloves, finely
    chopped
2 tablespoons Smoked
    tomato hot sauce (page 76)
    or hot sauce
¼ teaspoon ground white
    pepper
½ teaspoon ground allspice
1 tablespoon Aleppo pepper
    flakes or dried chilli flakes
1 tablespoon smoked paprika
flaky sea salt
2–3 tablespoons
    pomegranate molasses
    (optional)
Toasted nuts (page 27), to
    serve
full-fat Greek yoghurt or soft
    labneh (page 25), to serve

The original dish Buran (see 'Lady Buran and the ubiquitous aubergine', opposite) has evolved from its tenth-century 'straightforward' fried vegetable form. By the 13th century, variant Burans with the word *maghmour* or 'buried' in use by now included meat and yoghurt or replaced the aubergine with gourd. The dish travelled to North Africa (*braniya*) and Spain (*alboronia*) and remains in both, in the latter without meat (perhaps due to Lenten culture). Elsewhere other vegetables were included too, such as squash and tomatoes. And today, ironically, Buran has morphed into a category of dishes widely attributed as Iranian cold vegetable specialities. Flying the flag is the infamous *badinjhan borani,* a mixture of aubergines, onions and yoghurt, not too different from its 13th century counterpart. While the original Buran no longer exists, it remains the precursor to today's boranis (and mutubals, page 156), and the now infamous moussaka, too.

The moussaka of the Levant is a meatless version known as *musaqa'a,* or 'the chilled' and still as maghmour for some (page 202), and consists of spiced smoky charred aubergines, chickpeas and tomatoes served cold. You'll often also find a version of the dish omitting the chickpeas and served with a drizzle of yoghurt, as in this recipe. Any leftovers make for a wonderful sandwich filling the following day.

Char the aubergines, pepper and tomatoes according to the instructions on page 22. You can do this step the day before making the musaqa'a.

Slice off the stems of the vegetables and slice the aubergines lengthways. Remove the seeds from the tomatoes and then finely chop.

Place a heavy-based pan over medium heat, pour in the oil, add the onion and fry for 3–4 minutes, until softened and translucent. Add the garlic and cook for a further minute, stirring often, then add in the prepared aubergines, pepper and tomatoes. Stir in the smoked tomato hot sauce and spices, and season with salt to taste. Reduce the heat to low and cook, covered, for about 45 minutes, or until the vegetables have completely softened and look as though they are melting into the oil. Mix in the pomegranate molasses, if using, to taste and set aside to cool. Serve at room temperature scattered with toasted nuts, and with yoghurt as a side or drizzled over the top.

LADY BURAN AND THE UBIQUITOUS AUBERGINE

Aside from wedding a ninth-century Baghdad caliph and for having *the* most 'lavish' wedding of the middle ages, Khadija, nicknamed Lady Buran, is also known for her aubergine (eggplant) spread... and the spread of aubergine into the Middle Eastern cooking repertoire and beyond. Today aubergines are the most commonly consumed vegetable in the Middle East, where you may often hear them referred to as the lord or master or sheikh of vegetables. However, take a caravan ride back to eighth- or ninth-century Baghdad, capital of the Abbasid caliphate, and aubergines were denounced due to their bitter taste (like 'a scorpion's sting', as a bedouin described them) and the belief they caused various ailments.

As renowned historian Charles Perry states in *Medieval Arab Cookery*: 'there is no record of eggplant in the Arab countries before the Islamic Period'. And while aubergines had been cultivated in Iran at an earlier though indeterminable date, it's widely acknowledged that they had been assimilated into the Abbasid cooking repertoire with the Islamic conquest of Iran in the seventh century. Some 125 years after Lady Buran's wedding, a pinch of aubergine-based recipes make an appearance in the earliest-existing culinary book in Arabic, Ibn Sayyar's tenth-century cookery book, *The Book of Dishes*. The book contained two recipes named for the Lady Buran entitled 'Badhiinjan Buran' or 'Buran's Eggplant'. Both of these recipes (page 146), though with slight variations to their cooking methods and flavourings, called for salting the sliced or gashed aubergines to remove bitterness, a technique considered to have been innovative at the time and likely the catalyst to the proliferation of the vegetable. Some 300 years later, another book, by the same name, delivered a feast of aubergine dishes, and the rest is history.

LADY BURAN'S STICKY BADHINJAN FINGERS

serves 6–8 as part of
a multi-course
menu
prep 10 minutes
cook 20 minutes

8 long and thin (Thai or
Japanese) aubergines
(eggplants), sliced in half
lengthways
1 tablespoon flaky sea salt
80 ml (2½ fl oz/⅓ cup)
Argan oil, plus 1 tablespoon
if needed
1 teaspoon caraway seeds,
toasted and lightly crushed
15 g (½ oz) piece ginger,
peeled and chopped
1–2 fresh red chillies,
thinly sliced
1 garlic clove, thinly sliced
2 tablespoons soy sauce
2 tablespoons date syrup or
pomegranate molasses
2 tablespoons verjuice or
cider vinegar
1 tablespoon nigella seeds
1 tablespoon sesame seeds,
toasted
handful coriander (cilantro),
roughly chopped
freshly ground black pepper
full-fat Greek yoghurt,
to serve

This recipe weaves together elements of the two Buran aubergine (eggplant) recipes that appeared in the tenth-century *Book of Dishes*. Note how basic the dish was in its debut – the first four ingredients were all that was called for, the second recipe requiring just the addition of walnuts – such a far cry from the aubergine's modern-day rich and varied existence. In medieval times, they advocated soaking aubergines in salted water before frying, to rid them of their bitterness. Today's varieties have been bred to be less bitter, but I find salting them just before cooking improves the texture and absorption of flavours. While I adore my aubergines smoked on the stovetop (a technique that apparently didn't come about until the 13th century), I will admit I have developed an affinity for their flavour-absorbing abilities when self-steamed or baked.

Salt the aubergines and leave to sit in a colander for 5 minutes. Heat the oil in a large non-stick frying pan over medium heat. Add the aubergines and fry, shaking the pan to prevent sticking, for 4–5 minutes until they start to brown. Pour in 75 ml (2½ fl oz) water, partially cover with the lid and simmer until the liquid has evaporated and the aubergines are completely soft. Reduce the heat to low and add the caraway seeds, ginger, chillies, garlic and 1 tablespoon oil if needed. Cook for a further 1–2 minutes, then pour in the soy sauce, date syrup and verjuice, and boil for 2–3 minutes to reduce the liquid to a sticky sauce.

Transfer to a serving plate and sprinkle over the nigella seeds, sesame seeds, chopped coriander and freshly ground black pepper. Serve immediately with yoghurt on the side.

SWISS CHARD & GRAPE BORANI

serves   8 as part of a
         multi-course menu
prep   10 minutes
cook   10 minutes

400 g (14 oz) Swiss chard,
   stalks removed, leaves
   finely chopped
½ tablespoon nigella seeds
½ teaspoon Aleppo pepper
   flakes or dried chilli flakes
½ teaspoon dried rose
   petals
flaky sea salt
2 tablespoons olive oil,
   plus extra to serve
zest of 1 orange
150 g (5½ oz) white seedless
   grapes, roughly chopped
60 g (2 oz) walnuts, roughly
   chopped
350 g (12½ oz) soft Labneh
   (page 25) or full-fat
   Greek yoghurt
warm Mini Arabic bread
   puffs (page 30)

Esfenej borani, a dish made from spinach, nuts and yoghurt, is popular all over the Middle East (page 156). In the Levant, Swiss chard stalks can be reserved, cooked and tossed through a simple *tarator* dressing, transforming it into borani's cousin, a mutabal or used to make Kuku (page 129).

Place a frying pan over medium heat, add the Swiss chard, nigella seeds, pepper flakes, rose petals and season with salt. Cook through, stirring often, for 4–5 minutes, or until the chard is wilted. Add the oil and orange zest, then toss in the grapes and walnuts. Set aside to cool.

In a mixing bowl, combine the labneh and 45 ml (1½ fl oz) water and season with salt to taste. Use a hand blender to blitz to form a frothy and pourable consistency.

To serve, pour half of the labneh mixture on to a serving platter followed by half of the chard mixture. Repeat. Serve either at room temperature or chilled with warm Arabic bread and a drizzle of olive oil.

BALLOONED POTATO BORANI

WITH TOMATO CHAKA SAUCE

serves 6–8 as part of a
multi-course menu
prep 15 minutes
cook 25 minutes

500 g (1 lb 2 oz) even-sized
potatoes, peeled and
sliced into 5 mm (¼ in)
lengths
rapeseed oil, for deep-frying
Cucumber and mint yoghurt
(omit the cucumber)
(page 81), to serve

for the tomato chaka sauce,
optional:
2 teaspoons olive oil
1 shallot, finely chopped
2 garlic cloves, finely
chopped
2.5 cm (1 in) piece ginger,
peeled and finely chopped
130 g (4½ oz) tomato
passata (tomato purée)
1 tablespoon smoked paprika
flaky sea salt and freshly
ground black pepper

A new-world ingredient, the potato diffused into the Middle East via Spain. Fries are an essential part of any Middle Eastern table. Traditionally, the potato slices in an Afghani potato borani are pan-fried, but not crisp. I have kept the flavouring and composition of the dish intact but taken inspiration from the French technique of *pommes soufflé* of double-frying the potatoes to create crisp, airy, ballooned chips. You will need a kitchen thermometer for the recipe as the temperature of the oil is crucial to achieving the ballooned potatoes. While not all potatoes will 'balloon' during the second frying they will still be crisp and delicious. You could serve the potato borani with hot sauce (page 76) if you have that on hand.

Fill a large pan with cold water and soak the potato slices for 10 minutes.

Meanwhile, make the sauce (if using). Place a large frying pan over medium-low heat, add the oil then sauté the shallot for 4–5 minutes until soft and translucent. Add the garlic and ginger, and cook for a further minute or so, then add the tomato passata, paprika and salt and pepper. Cook for 5–10 minutes, until thickened. Set aside.

Drain the potato slices and pat very dry with paper towels.

In a large, deep frying pan, pour in enough oil to come up to about 7 cm (2¾ in) and heat to 130°C/260°F. Fill a separate pan with the same amount of oil and heat, bringing the temperature to 180°C/365°F. Drop the potatoes into the pan set at the lower temperature, in batches, carefully shaking the pan to keep the oil agitated and stop the potatoes from sticking. Cook the potatoes for about 5 minutes, at which point they should start to blister. You don't want them to colour though, so monitor the heat level. As soon as you start to see some raised skin on them, use a slotted spoon and, working with only one at a time, drop the blistering potato into the second pan with the hotter oil. Cook for 1–2 minutes, until crisp, golden and ballooned. Remove with a slotted spoon and transfer to a paper-towel-lined plate. Repeat the process with the remaining potatoes.

To serve, spread half the yoghurt over a warm serving dish, then dollop over some of the tomato sauce. Arrange the potatoes on top and lightly drizzle with extra yoghurt and sauce, or serve the sauces on the side.

PUMPKIN & POMELO BORANI

WITH COCONUT TARATOR

serves 4–6 as part of a multi-course menu
prep 20 minutes
cook 35 minutes

1.5 kg (3 lb 5 oz) mixed squash and pumpkin, preferably heirloom, cut into 2 cm (¾ in) wedges
flaky sea salt and freshly ground black pepper
2 tablespoons olive oil
1 pomelo or grapefruit, peeled, deseeded and divided into large chunks
1 red chilli, thinly sliced
2–3 tablespoons dried chickpeas (page 72) or cooked chickpeas
3–4 tablespoons shredded coconut
1 tablespoon roughly chopped mint
1 tablespoon roughly chopped coriander (cilantro)

for the coconut and pomelo tarator:
100 ml (3½ fl oz) coconut milk
2 garlic cloves, finely chopped
3–4 tablespoons honey, plus extra to taste
2 tablespoons pomelo or grapefruit juice
flaky sea salt and freshly ground black pepper

I adore coconut, which is an ingredient of the Persian/Central Asian kitchen, and especially love it with pumpkin. Here, it complements the dish beautifully without overpowering the other ingredients. This borani is also delicious served with the Tomato chaka sauce on page 149.

A tarator is a dressing. Though this one is less typical, the classic is a combination of tahini, garlic and lemon juice – a traditional dressing for salads or mutabals.

Preheat the oven to 200°C/400°F/Gas 6.

Put the squash and pumpkin on a baking sheet. Sprinkle with salt and pepper and drizzle with the oil. Bake for 30–35 minutes, until tender.

Meanwhile, make the tarator. Whisk together the coconut milk, garlic, honey, pomelo juice and salt and pepper. Taste and adjust seasoning, adding more honey if you'd like it sweeter.

Once the pumpkin is tender and cooked through, remove from the oven and transfer to a serving platter along with the pomelo. Drizzle over the tarator and sprinkle over the chilli, the dried chickpeas, the shredded coconut, the herbs and season with freshly ground pepper. Serve warm.

THE IMAM FAINTED

serves   6-8
prep   30 minutes
cook   1 hour

1 kg (2 lb 3 oz) (or about
  20) baby aubergines
  (eggplants), sliced in half
  lengthways, stalks intact
flaky sea salt
120 ml (4 fl oz/½ cup) olive
  oil, or more as needed

for the filling:
2 tablespoons extra virgin
  olive oil
1 small onion, finely chopped
50 g (1¾ oz) green (bell)
  pepper, finely chopped
  (optional)
1-2 Scotch bonnet chillies,
  finely chopped (optional)
2 garlic cloves, finely
  chopped
1 kg (2 lb 3 oz) tomatoes,
  peeled, deseeded and
  finely chopped or 700 g
  (1 lb 9 oz) tinned
  chopped tomatoes
flaky sea salt

to serve:
extra virgin olive oil
1-2 tablespoons chopped
  parsley
2 tablespoons pine nuts,
  toasted
Cucumber and mint yoghurt
  (page 81), or full-fat Greek
  yoghurt (optional)

The Turkish name of this dish, *Imam Biyaldi,* translates to 'the imam fainted' and I've heard anything from 'the imam fainted because the dish was so delicious' to 'he fainted due to the sheer amount of olive oil used in the dish'. I don't think anyone really knows from what or why the imam fainted – or if he really ever did at all – though certainly my version is not for the faint-hearted thanks to the Scotch bonnet chillies.

Gently puncture the cut (white) sides of the aubergines several times with a fork, being careful not to go so deep as to puncture the skins. Sprinkle the cut-sides with a pinch of salt and set aside in a colander for about 20 minutes. Give the aubergines a squeeze, rinse in water, drain and pat dry with paper towels.

Preheat the oven to 170°C/340°F/Gas 3. Grease a casserole dish with oil.

Heat the oil in a large frying pan over medium-high heat. When hot, add the aubergines, cut-sides down and in batches to avoid overcrowding, and fry for 3-4 minutes, until golden and cooked through. Turn over and brown the skin sides for a few minutes. Transfer to a plate, placing the aubergines cut-side up. Leave until cool enough to handle, then use a spoon to scoop out the flesh from the aubergines, starting from the base and working up to the stalks, and reserve. Discard any seeds and be extra careful and try not to pierce the skins. Arrange the aubergine skins in the prepared dish.

Meanwhile, make the filling. Place a frying pan over medium-high heat, add the extra virgin olive oil and the onion, and cook for 10-15 minutes, until translucent. Next, add the pepper and chillies (if using), and cook for 2-3 minutes, stirring often. Stir in the garlic and cook for a further minute. Add the tomatoes, season with salt and simmer until the mixture has thickened, about 10 minutes. Stir often to prevent the mixture from catching.

Add the aubergine flesh and stir. Add about a teaspoon of the tomato mixture to each aubergine skin. Cover with foil and bake for around 20-30 minutes, or until meltingly soft. Remove them from the oven and leave to cool. Transfer to a serving plate and drizzle generously with extra virgin olive oil, just to give them a little bit more of a shine. Serve at room temperature garnished with parsley and pine nuts and, if you like, some cucumber and mint yoghurt.

WHO GIVES A TOSS? HUMMUS, MUTABAL AND BORANI

While you may be familiar with mutabal as 'aubergine (eggplant) dip' (see also page 158), there is a garden to weed through. While 'hummus' obviously means chickpea (if you speak Arabic) – and it's not a hummus if you don't use any – and boranis are obviously descendants of Lady Buran's eggplant (page 146), then what the toss does mutabal mean? Mutabal, occasionally 'mispopularised' as baba ghanoush (page 158), is not a word for one unique dish. Rather, it is a verb representing a tribe of dishes, generally based on a common technique – that of 'giving a toss' in fact. The word *mutabal* in Arabic can imply a number of actions depending on its usage, namely 'seasoned', 'dressed', 'tossed', 'marinated' or 'spiced'. The actual marinade or seasoning is referred to as 'tetbeeleh' or 'tebil' (a spice mix) and the final dish is the mutabal, implying either 'tossed' or 'marinated' depending on the instance.

Aubergine mutabal is the most well-known dish, but in fact the possibilities are measureless. A purée consistency is not defining. Ingredients may be raw, fried, sliced, mashed, whipped or dressed or emulsified in oil, garlic, lemon, vinaigrette, yoghurt or tahini, paired with aubergine to courgettes (zucchinis), cauliflower, beetroot (beets) and of course bean and pulse varieties, including the Beyoncé of mutabals – hummus. It's not just vegetables and pulses that get to play 'dress up' or 'toss up'. Meat too gets the tossing action. And let's not neglect the now infamous Levantine salad tabbouleh (page 166). So, next time you purée or toss, add a tarator (page 150) or go all-yoghurt, consider using the word mutabal (Arab/Levantine) or perhaps borani (Central Asian) rather than hummus when chickpeas don't star.

AUBERGINE MUTABAL

serves 8 as part of
        a multi-course
        menu
prep   5 minutes
cook   45 minutes

750 g (1 lb 11 oz) (about 2–3)
   aubergines (eggplants)
1 tablespoon tahini
1 garlic clove, crushed to a
   paste
2 tablespoons verjuice or
   cider vinegar
4 tablespoons soft Labneh
   (page 25) or full-fat Greek
   yoghurt
flaky sea salt
1 tablespoon Smoked tomato
   hot sauce (page 76) or hot
   sauce, mixed with
   1 tablespoon water
1 x quantity Tempura onions
   (page 23)
Aysh pita pyramids (page 31)
   or Mini Arabic bread puffs
   (page 30), to
   serve (optional)

In Syria there are variations on the aubergine mutabal, known as *mutabal hamawi* (a speciality of the city of Hama) or *batirish/batarsh*, where minced (ground) meat is added. The aubergines may be smoked or fried and tahini needn't always feature. Often it's tossed with vinegar or yoghurt and garnished with pomegranate seeds.

Aubergine mutabal is often confused with baba ghanoush, which in Syria is a salsa-like chopped aubergine dish, and in Lebanon it is also known as Monk's Salad (*salatet el raheb*). Along the diffusion road, baba ghanoush in the West became associated with this dip.

Char the aubergines according to the instructions on page 22 and place the peeled and drained flesh in a mixing bowl. Add the tahini, garlic, verjuice and 1 tablespoon of the yoghurt. Season to taste with salt. Toss the mixture together using a fork for a more rustic texture or use a pestle and mortar if you're after a creamier consistency. It's meant to have some body, so don't purée it completely.

Mix the remaining yoghurt with 1 tablespoon of water to form a pourable consistency.

Transfer the mixture to two small serving bowls or one large one and create a shallow well in the middle. Drizzle over the hot sauce and remaining yoghurt and, if not serving it immediately, cover and place in the fridge. Just before serving, bring back to room temperature and pile the tempura onions in a mound on top. Serve with bread and Plated garden (page 75), if you like.

Also try: Add about 100 g (3½ oz) cooked and spiced minced lamb as a layer between the shatta and the tempura onions.

BEETROOT MUTABAL

WITH APPLE, WALNUTS & ANCHOVY OIL

serves   6-8 as part of
          a multi-course
          menu
prep   10 minutes
cook   45 minutes

400 g (3-4 small) beetroot
   (beets), unpeeled
   and washed
1 green apple
2 tablespoons roughly
   chopped walnuts
zest and juice of 1 grapefruit
60-75 ml (2-2½ fl oz) tahini
½ teaspoon ground cumin
1 garlic clove, finely chopped
1-2 tablespoons soft Labneh
   (page 28) or full-fat Greek
   yoghurt (optional)
flaky sea salt and freshly
   ground black pepper
Aysh pita pyramids (page
   31) or Mini Arabic bread
   puffs (page 30), to serve
   (optional)

for the anchovy oil:
125 ml (4 fl oz/½ cup) olive
   oil
1 anchovy, tinned in oil

This is what usually gets passed off as beetroot 'hummus' when, essentially, it is a mutabal. Although there is tahini in it, if there are no chickpeas, it's not a hummus!

Fill a large saucepan with salted water, add the beetroot and bring to the boil over high heat. Reduce the heat and simmer, covered, for 30-45 minutes, or until tender when pierced with a knife. Remove from the heat, drain, roughly chop and set the beets aside in a mixing bowl.

Meanwhile, make the anchovy oil. Place a frying pan over medium heat, add the oil and anchovy, and heat through, just until the anchovy is beginning to brown and sizzle. Transfer to a small food blender and blitz. Set aside.

Core and cut the apples into matchsticks and toss with the walnuts in a mixing bowl, add the grapefruit zest and 1-2 tablespoons of its juice.

Add the tahini, cumin, and garlic – and labneh if using – to the bowl with the beetroot. Using a hand blender, blitz to a purée, adding the remaining grapefruit juice to form a spreadable consistency. Season with salt and pepper, taste and adjust as needed.

Transfer the beetroot mixture to two shallow serving bowls or one large one, and create a shallow well in the middle. Fill with the apple and walnut mixture. Drizzle over the anchovy oil and serve immediately. Alternatively, if making in advance, place in the fridge and bring back to room temperature before serving. Serve with Arabic pyramids or bread, if you like.

AVOCADO MUTABAL

WITH PEACH & POMEGRANATE

serves   6–8 as part of
        a multi-course
        menu
prep   10 minutes

650 g (1 lb 7 oz) ripe
   avocados
flaky sea salt and freshly
   ground black pepper
juice of 2–3 limes
60 ml (2 fl oz/¼ cup) tahini
Aysh pita pyramids (page 31)
   or Mini Arabic bread puffs
   (page 30), to
   serve (optional)

for the peach and
pomegranate topping:
1 peach, stone removed
   and diced
½ red onion, finely chopped
1 red chilli, finely chopped
seeds of ½ pomegranate
1–2 tablespoons finely
   chopped coriander
   (cilantro)
flaky sea salt and freshly
   ground black pepper

If Arabs were to make guacamole, it would be a mutabal or borani. Everyone thinks of tomatoes as the first addition to guacamole. I've always preferred mine with papaya or mango. Here, I offer up another stone fruit as an option: peach. You can also use loquat. This is sure to shake up every guacamole lover out there. See photo on pages 162–163.

Cut the avocados in half and remove the stones. Scoop the flesh out into a mixing bowl and add some of the lime juice. Mash with a fork and season with salt and pepper, and more lime juice if needed. The mixture should be slightly sharp.

Whisk the tahini to get rid of any clumps and then fold into the avocado. Mix well and adjust the seasoning to taste.

In a separate bowl, make the topping. Toss the peach, onion, chilli, pomegranate seeds, half the coriander and season with salt and pepper and any remaining lime juice.

Transfer the avocado mixture to two small serving bowls or one large one, and create a shallow well in the middle. Spoon over the fruit mixture, then sprinkle with the remaining coriander. Serve slightly chilled with bread and a Plated garden (page 75), if you like.

BROAD BEAN MUTABAL

serves 4-8 as part of
a multi-course
menu
prep 15 minutes
cook 30 minutes

750 g (1 lb 11 oz) fresh broad
beans (fava beans), sliced
into slivers, or 500 g
(1 lb 2 oz) frozen
podded beans
3-4 garlic cloves, finely
chopped
handful coriander (cilantro)
leaves, finely chopped
75 ml (2½ fl oz) olive oil
juice of 1 lemon
flaky sea salt and freshly
ground black pepper
Mini Arabic bread puffs
(page 30), to serve
(optional)

The Levantine *tetbeeleh* is a heady combination of coriander, garlic, lemon juice and olive oil. This dressing is tossed with a host of vegetables such as blanched green beans, potato and beetroot or mixed pulses. Here's one way with it.

When we pick broad beans fresh from the garden in the spring, we tend to use the broad beans still in their tender pods, chopped into slivers. You can try it too if you have access to fresh, homegrown broad beans. Otherwise, use frozen podded beans.

Place the broad beans in a heavy-based saucepan with 500 ml (17 fl oz/ 2 cups) water, season with salt, cover and bring to the boil over high heat. Reduce the heat and simmer for about 20 minutes, or until soft but slightly al dente. Add the garlic and cook through for a further 2-3 minutes. Stir in the coriander, cover and cook for a further 5 minutes. Remove from the heat, drizzle over the oil and lemon juice, then season with salt and pepper to taste. Serve warm with Arabic bread, if you like.

Also try: For a more substantial serving, toss in some Bacon basturma (page 95) or cooked chorizo, and serve with yoghurt.

CARROT & CARAWAY MUTABAL

WITH CASHEW & DATE BROWNED BUTTER

serves 6–8 as part of
a multi-course
menu
prep   10 minutes
cook   20–25 minutes

500 g (1 lb 2 oz) carrots,
peeled and roughly
chopped
½ teaspoon caraway seeds
2–3 tablespoons tahini
juice of 1 lemon
Aysh pita pyramids (page 31)
or pita crisps, to serve
(optional)
flaky sea salt and freshly
ground black pepper

for the topping:
75 g (2¾ oz) butter
45 g (1½ oz/¼ cup) raw
unsalted cashews
60 g (2 oz/⅓ cup) pitted
dates, finely chopped
pinch of ground cinnamon
2 tablespoons
shredded coconut

This is an absolute stunner of a dip – the bowl has never failed to be wiped clean.

Fill a large pan with salted water and add the carrots. Bring to the boil over high heat and cook for 10 minutes, or until very tender. Drain well.

Heat a small frying pan and toast the caraway seeds until aromatic. Remove from the heat and set aside.

In a food processor or using a hand blender, blitz the carrots with the caraway seeds. Add the tahini and lemon juice, and season to taste with salt.

Divide the carrot mutabal between two serving bowls. Using a spoon, make a well in the centre. Set aside while you make the topping.

Melt the butter in a small frying pan over medium heat, until bubbling, then add the cashews and toss to coat. Fry for 1–2 minutes, tossing often, until the cashews are light golden brown in colour and the butter nicely browned. Remove from the heat, add the dates and cinnamon and stir well.

Spoon half the mixture into the well of each serving bowl, drizzling over the browned butter. Sprinkle with the shredded coconut and serve immediately with Arabic Pita pyramids, if you like.

ON THE TABBOULEH TRAIL

Tabbouleh is widely proclaimed to have originated in the mountains of Lebanon and Syria with an inherent confusion: is it a grain or herb salad? That depends on who you are asking. Cuisine in the region is not dictated by national boundaries. Rather, common themes stretch across borders, influenced by terroir and religion. Ask a Lebanese and they'll shake a bundle of parsley and mint at you as they proclaim that a true tabbouleh is one that is herb based.

The Turkish word for the dish, *kısır*, insinuates 'infertile', 'barren' or 'lacking', perhaps applied because of the salad's lack of meat. As does the Armenian nickname for the dish, *sud khaymeh*, i.e. a meatless or mock 'steak tartare'. This is also perhaps telling of tabbouleh's origins. It may have begun as the region's tartares – in the kofte/kebbeh theme – and as it wound through the burghul belt the proportions of grain to meat changed over time, probably influenced by austerity and lenten culture. A modern parallel is with the Turkish tartare known as *çiğ köfte*, believed to be of Kurdish origin, which involves lean mince kneaded with fine burghul, pepper, tomato paste, onion and spices, much like the Arab *kebbeh nayye*. A mock or vegan çiğ köfte is now the commercially preferred option, again due to austerity as well as modern food safety regulations. As further evidence, the region's tartares – much like tabbouleh – are often served in or alongside lettuce cups or vine leaves and have traditionally dotted the mezze table to help soak up raki or arak.

Another proportion drift was inspired by the 'refined' city ladies of Beirut who would reverse the ratio of burghul to parsley (often noted and admonished by Syrians) both to lessen burghul's renowned 'bloating' effect and perhaps as a status symbol. In fact, it is acknowledged that even by Lebanese standards, tabbouleh traditionally had more burghul than the modern-day national dish offers up. Of course, in diaspora, one could not find burghul easily (such was the case when my father briefly resided in the US in the 1980s), which has also fed the evolution and the use of couscous as a replacement for that matter.

There are some interesting tabbouleh variations. In parts of Lebanon and Syria there exists a vaguely known, seasonal tabbouleh that is made from cabbage. Syrian, Turkish and Armenian 'tabbouleh' recipes are often labelled as *tabbouleh hamra* or red tabbouleh and may include crushed pepper flakes, sumac, pomegranate molasses, allspice, or a combination of baharat (page 33) as well as pomegranate seeds, cucumber and green pepper.

WINTER TABBOULEH

WITH APPLE & TOASTED CHESTNUT

serves 4–6
prep   15 minutes

500 g (1 lb 2 oz) white
  cabbage, thinly shredded
1 garlic clove, finely chopped
½ teaspoon dried mint
1–2 apples, cored and
  roughly chopped
75 g (2¾ oz) toasted
  chestnuts, chopped
seeds of 1 pomegranate
2–3 tablespoons olive oil
1–2 tablespoons verjuice or
  cider vinegar
flaky sea salt and freshly
  ground black pepper

In Syria and parts of Lebanon, namely in the Bekaa Valley and nearer to the Syrian border, it is popular to prepare a salad with shredded cabbage in the winter, when fresh parsley and tomatoes are not at their seasonal best. It receives the apt label of white tabbouleh. I am fond of nicknaming my salads after seasons, so my version shall be winter tabbouleh. It is an unrelenting crowd-charmer and it will please the cook too, since it's a lot easier to prepare than the all-star tabbouleh.

Apples and chestnuts are a traditional seasonal combination in Lebanon if not a classical addition to tabbouleh, but they set this salad apart.

Combine the ingredients in a mixing bowl. Taste to adjust the seasoning and serve.

Also try: This is faultlessly delicious with some cooked Puy lentils or green lentils tossed in.

OLD-COUNTRY TABBOULEH

serves 4–6
prep   30 minutes
cook   10 minutes

300 g (10½ oz) fine burghul
3 tomatoes
2 fresh green chillies
125 ml (4 fl oz/½ cup)
   olive oil
5–6 spring onions (scallions),
   thinly sliced
handful parsley leaves,
   finely chopped
3 tablespoons finely
   chopped mint
2 teaspoons Aleppo pepper
   flakes or dried chilli flakes
2 teaspoons ground cumin
1 teaspoon smoked paprika
3 tablespoons pomegranate
   molasses
flaky sea salt and freshly
   ground black pepper
baby gem lettuce leaves,
   to serve

For this salad, try to use fine burghul to yield the traditional texture. If you're short on time, you could opt to use tomato paste and/or pepper paste en lieu of smoking the chillies and tomatoes. Sometimes I've even use Smoked tomato hot sauce (page 76) and have tossed in whatever herbs I have in the fridge along with cucumbers and pomegranate seeds. This is lovely paired with the winter tabbouleh (page 168) for a dinner party.

Place the burghul in a bowl with 375 ml (12½ fl oz/1½ cups) just-boiled water, add a pinch of salt, stir, cover and soak for 10–15 minutes.

Char the tomatoes and chillies, and peel them, following the instructions on page 26. Finely chop the flesh to near paste and then add to the burghul. Stir together, adding oil as you go. Toss in the remaining ingredients, season with salt and pepper, taste and adjust accordingly. Serve warm or at room temperature.

Also try: You can bulk this up by adding cooked chickpeas, or try it with Bacon basturma (page 95) or chorizo tossed in.

WILL THE REAL HUMMUS PLEASE STAND UP?

The word *hummus* literally means 'chickpea' in Arabic, while in the West it has become the golden pass-par-tout name to attach to dips of all sorts, chickpea included or not. For the last decade, hummus has been a 'health' food trend in the West, and it seems that if tahini is added to a puréed vegetable, the word hummus is its automatic classification. But the dip liberally referred to as 'hummus' is inspired by the dish we, in the Middle East, call *hummus bi tahini* and *both* chickpeas and tahini must be present. You can omit the tahini and still call it hummus. But if it's another pulse or vegetable mixed with tahini then we're definitely not talking hummus and we're likely in the domain of mutabal or borani (page 156).

Hummus is such a staple in the Middle East that there are dedicated hummus and *ful* (broad bean/fava) shops, called *hamsani* or *fawal*. Here, they serve up a variety of delights: the velvet-smooth 'whipped' paste (hummus bi tahini) topped or plain, chunky (*hummus msabaha*) and brothy (*hummus balila*) versions and sometimes a mix of chickpeas and broad beans (fava beans) (*hummus bi ful*) – all served either hot or at room temperature, mainly for breakfast but equally popular at lunch.

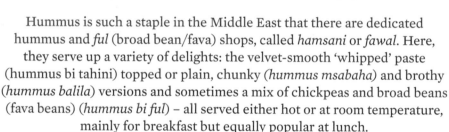

So who then owns hummus? No one! It is clear the chickpea and its purée has long been ubiquitous in the region where the pulse has been found in Bronze Age deposits in Jericho and Babylon, modern-day Palestine and Iraq.

Recipes for a precursor to hummus appear in two 13th-century cookbooks, one from Cairo, where vinegar is used, and one from Syria, which called for mashing the chickpeas with lemon. Tahini (though an ancient ingredient itself) does not appear to be documented in hummus until an 18th-century Damascene recipe. I'm of the belief that hummus bi tahini must have a longer, rooted history that is simply unwritten.

NOTES ON HUMMUS

A staple hummus bi tahini is made up of three hallmark ingredients: hummus or chickpeas, tahini and lemon juice. One can then add garlic and spices, and toppings to make it go further. The spices should be used sparingly though, and if adding garlic go easy.

CHOOSE YOUR CHICKPEA

Whatever you do, try to avoid using tinned chickpeas for hummus. If available, look out for garbanzos (some producers label these 'jumbo chickpeas'). They are not entirely the same as chickpeas (desi varieties) but rather more plump in 'caliber', offering up more 'pulse mass' to skin which is also softer and easier to peel as well as being whiter in colour – making for a creamier and cream-coloured hummus. These are often preferred in the Middle East for the making of hummus.

There is also the peeled variety, which I always keep on hand and favour because they require no soaking and obviously no peeling and cook in a jiffy. They are more expensive though and you may need to place an order from a speciality store (I order them from a Greek producer). They are excellent used in a whipped hummus where a smooth and velvety texture is ideal. If you are pushed for time and want to ignore all warnings and use tinned chickpeas, be sure to soak them in water for 10 minutes and then rinse them well before using to remove their 'tin' flavour.

METHOD IN MADNESS

To hasten the cooking process of the chickpeas, add a large pinch of bicarbonate of soda (baking soda) when soaking them the night before using. Be sure to rinse the chickpeas well before cooking.

I recommend peeling the chickpeas once cooked. This sounds arduous, but it's actually quite a simple process of rinsing them under cold water a few times once cooked, to loosen the skins. Trust me, it will guarantee you a smooth, creamy hummus. The other trick if you really can't be bothered with peeling is to add a couple of ice cubes when you're puréeing the chickpeas to help break them down (always before adding the tahini otherwise the texture will turn grainy).

It's also worth saving about 60 ml (2 fl oz/¼ cup) of the cooked chickpea liquid (AKA aquafaba) to use if you'd like to obtain an airy texture in your hummus. Simply whip the aquafaba to soft peaks and stir through.

BE SELECTIVE IN THE CHOICE OF FAT

Hummus purists will only use one kind of fat in whipped hummus, tahini. However, there is a trend amongst restaurants to use oil because it's cheaper than tahini and lends an airier texture. I find the taste washed out. I am open to the idea that you can use alternative quality fats, such a butter (page 174), but just make sure it's the only fat that is going into the hummus.

WHIPPED HUMMUS

serves   6–8 as part of
         a multi-course
         menu
prep   20 minutes, plus
         overnight soaking
cook   1 hour

250 g (9 oz) dried chickpeas,
   ideally jumbo garbanzo
   (or 1 x 400 g (14 oz) tin
   chickpeas, drained
   and rinsed)
pinch of bicarbonate of soda
   (baking soda)
1 garlic clove, crushed
   (optional)
flaky sea salt
2–3 small ice cubes
90 ml (3 fl oz) tahini
75 ml (2½ fl oz) lemon juice,
   plus extra to taste
pinch of ground allspice

This is a basic hummus recipe. It is very versatile and you can add toppings or flavourings as you wish. If you've managed to find the peeled variety there is no need to soak them first. Just cook them according to packet instructions. Always serve your hummus at room temperature or – if you've just made it – warm.

Place the chickpeas in a large bowl with plenty of water. Add the bicarbonate of soda and leave the chickpeas to soak overnight.

The next day, rinse the soaked chickpeas well under cold running water and place in a saucepan. Cover with water, bring to the boil over medium-high heat, then reduce the heat to low. Partially cover the pan and cook for 30 minutes, then fully cover and cook for a further 1 hour, or until very tender. Skim off any scum that forms on the surface with a spoon.

Drain the chickpeas, then loosen their skins by rinsing them under cold water several times. Cover the chickpeas with water and swish them with your hands several times to loosen any skins. Discard the skins and drain.

Place the chickpeas, garlic (if using) and pinch of salt in a food processor along with the ice cubes and pulse to a smooth paste, stopping to scrape down the mixture from the edges of the food processor every so often.

Meanwhile, whisk the tahini, lemon juice and 1 tablespoon cold water in a bowl until well incorporated. Pour in the tahini and lemon mixture along with the allspice and pulse again until it forms a smooth, well-blended purée. Taste and adjust the seasoning, if needed, then pulse for about 1 minute until well incorporated. If the hummus is too thick, add a little more lemon juice and/or water (careful not to dilute the zesty flavours).

Transfer the hummus to a large, shallow serving bowl. Make a crater in the centre of the hummus. Serve as is or with toppings (pages 173–180).

butter hummus variation: Prepare the hummus according to recipe until the chickpeas have been pulsed with the ice cubes to form a smooth paste. In a bowl, whisk together 100 g (3½ oz) melted butter with 2–3 tablespoons of the chickpea cooking water (see aquafaba, page 171) until well incorporated then pour into the hummus mixture until combined. Use this for the recipe on page 180.

MOCK HUMMUS

WITH ZA'ATAR PESTO & SUN-DRIED TOMATOES

serves   6–8 as part of
         a multi-course
         menu
prep   10 minutes
cook   30–45 minutes

225 g (8 oz) butter beans
  (lima beans), soaked and
  boiled till soft (or 1 x 400g
  /14 oz tin, drained and
  rinsed)
1–2 garlic cloves, roughly
  chopped
1–2 ice cubes
2–3 tablespoons tahini
juice of 1–2 lemons
flaky sea salt
pinch of allspice
2 tablespoons Spiked za'atar
  and almond pesto
  (page 87) diluted with
  4 tablespoons olive oil
5–6 sun-dried tomatoes,
  thinly sliced

I'm offering up an option of hummus here that is almost hard to distinguish as hummus. A mutabal at heart, traditionally it is rustic-smooth, dressed with loads of garlic, lemon and fresh coriander as in the broad bean mutabal (page 161). This really tastes as if you were having hummus – I bet you a bag of chickpeas no one will know! An excellent recipe to have on hand should the supermarket run out of chickpeas. I've topped the mixture with a za'atar pesto and sun-dried tomatoes. In fact, it's great to make this if you're short on time, since butter beans cook quicker than chickpeas and cream nicely. Less hassle. Reduce the garlic, if you like.

Add the butter beans, garlic and 1–2 ice cubes to a food processor. Pulse to a fine paste. Add the tahini, juice of 1 lemon, salt, allspice and pulse once more to incorporate. Taste and adjust seasoning, adding more lemon to your liking. Transfer the butter bean mixture to two small serving bowls or one large one and create a shallow well in the middle. Drizzle over the za'atar pesto and sprinkle over the sun-dried tomatoes.

WHIPPED HUMMUS

WITH ROAST BEETROOT & FENNEL

serves 6–8 as part of
a multi-course
menu
prep 15 minutes
cook 30–35 minutes

300 g (10½ oz) (roughly 2)
mixed candied, orange or
regular beetroot (beets),
peeled and cut into
small wedges or cubes
olive oil, for drizzling
1 x quantity Whipped
hummus (page 174)

for the dried lime oil:
2 dried limes
1 teaspoon fennel seeds
¼ teaspoon cumin seeds
100 ml (3½ fl oz) olive oil

I often see recipes labelled as beetroot 'hummus' when there are no chickpeas in the mix. A correlation to hummus is mistakingly made because the beetroot has been puréed and tahini used, which I have no doubt is still delicious, but it makes it a beetroot mutabal (page 159). This here is a true beetroot hummus and while you could purée it, I prefer the contrast of textures, colours and temperatures.

Dried lime is used here to lend a sharp, astringent flavour. If you can't find it use fresh lime or grapefruit juice. If making the Dried lime oil, do so at least a day in advance to allow the spices to infuse.

Preheat the oven to 200°C/400°F/Gas 6.

Place the beetroot in a sheet of foil, season with a little salt and drizzle with oil, then gather the foil together to make a parcel. Seal well. Transfer the parcel to a baking sheet and bake for 30 minutes, or until just tender. Remove and set aside to cool.

Meanwhile, use a heavy knife to smash the dried limes, remove the seeds and discard and place the dried lime shells in a small frying pan with the fennel and cumin seeds. Set over medium heat and toast, stirring often, for about 1 minute or until the aromas are released from the spices. Remove from the heat and then pour over the oil. Stir well and set aside.

Pour the oil through a fine sieve into a mixing bowl and add the cooked beetroot. Mix together.

Divide the whipped hummus between two shallow serving bowls, make a crater in the centre of the hummus and top with the beetroot. Drizzle over the residual oil from the bowl and serve warm, with Arabic bread, if you like.

WHIPPED HUMMUS

WITH OSSO BUCCO & DATES

serves 6-8 as part of
        a multi-course
        menu
prep   15 minutes
cook   2½-3 hours

20 g (¾ oz) butter
750 g (1 lb 11 oz) veal shank
    or oxtail
½ tablespoon ground ginger
½ teaspoon ground white
    pepper
1 teaspoon ground cinnamon
1 teaspoon ground coriander
1 teaspoon ground allspice
½ teaspoon ground mace
3 garlic cloves, finely
    chopped
1 leek, thinly sliced
2 celery stalks, thinly sliced
1 carrot, thinly sliced
1 red onion, thickly sliced
50 g (2 oz/¼ cup) pitted
    dates
2 bay leaves
1 bone marrow (optional)
250 ml (8½ fl oz/1 cup)
    white wine
500 ml (17 fl oz/2 cups)
    beef stock or water
flaky sea salt
1 x quantity Whipped
    hummus (page 174)

Is there anything better than hummus topped with a slow-cooked meaty stew? I love the flavours in this winter-warmer, which transforms hummus into a substantial and satiating meal. The sharpness from the lemon in the hummus is particularly important here to cut through the richness of the stew.

Preheat the oven to 160°C/320°F/Gas 2.

Melt half the butter in a heavy-based an ovenproof saucepan over medium heat. Add the veal shank and brown on all sides, turning every so often, for 8–10 minutes. Sprinkle over the spices, toss to combine, then transfer to a plate and set aside.

Melt the remaining butter in the pan over low heat, then add the garlic, leek, celery and carrot. Cover and allow to sweat for 5–6 minutes, stirring occasionally. Transfer the vegetables to a plate, then add the onion to the pan, stirring to combine. Cover and cook for 5–7 minutes, until slightly softened. Return the shank and vegetables to the pan along with the dates, bay leaves and, if using, marrow bone. Pour in the wine, bring to the boil over high heat and cook for a further 2 minutes. Pour in the stock and season with salt. Cover and place in the oven to cook for 2–3 hours, until the sauce has thickened and the shank is tender at the touch of a fork.

Divide the whipped hummus between two shallow serving bowls, make a crater in the centre of the hummus and top with the stew. Serve warm.

BUTTER HUMMUS

WITH BRAISED BROCCOLI, GARLIC & CHILLI

serves   6–8 as part of
         a multi-course
         menu
prep   15 minutes
cook   10 minutes

150 g (5½ oz) broccoli,
  broken into florets
4 tablespoons Aged butter
  (page 27) or butter
4 garlic cloves, very thinly
  sliced
handful almonds, halved
1 red chilli, thinly sliced
zest of ¼ grapefruit, cut into
  fine matchsticks
handful parsley, roughly
  chopped
1 x quantity Butter hummus
  (see variation, page 174)

Fact: butter does make everything taste better. This dish is
a wonderful example of how being selective with the fat chosen
can make a whipped hummus shine. Make the butter hummus
according to the recipe on page 174.

Bring a saucepan of water to the boil and blanch the broccoli for
4 minutes, until just tender. Drain and set aside.

Melt the butter in a frying pan over medium heat. Add the garlic,
almonds and chilli and cook for a minute, until the almonds are slightly
golden in colour. Add the broccoli and grapefruit zest, and cook for
a further 3–4 minutes.

Divide the butter hummus between two shallow serving bowls, make
a crater in the centre of the hummus and top with the broccoli and
almonds. Drizzle over the butter residue in the pan and sprinkle with
the chopped parsley. Serve immediately.

HUMMUS 'BROTH'

WITH SEARED TUNA & EGG

serves 4
prep 10 minutes
cook 45 minutes

80 ml (2½ fl oz/⅓ cup)
  olive oil
1 large onion, finely chopped
4 garlic cloves, finely
  chopped
1 tablespoon ground
  turmeric
1 teaspoon ground ginger
2 teaspoons ground cumin
1 teaspoon paprika
flaky sea salt
400 g (14 oz) cooked
  chickpeas (or 1 x 400 g/
  14 oz tin of chickpeas,
  drained and rinsed)
80 ml (2½ fl oz/⅓ cup)
  Smoked tomato hot sauce
  (page 78) or hot sauce,
  to taste
1.5 litres (51 fl oz/6 cups)
  vegetable stock or water
handful chopped coriander
  (cilantro), plus extra to
  garnish
1 x 240 g (8½ oz) tuna steak
2 tablespoons capers
1 lime, cut into wedges
4 hard-boiled eggs, peeled
  and cut into quarters
12–15 black olives, pitted
  (optional)

This Tunisian stew is for anyone that loves a Niçoise salad but yearns for a dash of warmth and heartiness too. Though most often enjoyed for breakfast or brunch, it will not disappoint no matter the hour. Adjust hot sauce measurements based on heat tolerance.

Add 65 ml (2¼ fl oz) of the oil to a deep, wide pan and place over medium heat. Add the onion and cook, covered and stirring often, for 3–5 minutes. Add the garlic, stir for a minute, then add the spices, chickpeas and hot sauce, and toss to coat. Pour in the stock, season with salt to taste, add the coriander and bring to the boil. Reduce the heat to medium-low, cover and simmer for 30–40 minutes, until the chickpeas are incredibly tender and the broth has thickened.

Lightly grease a griddle pan with the remaining oil and place over high heat. When the pan is smoking hot, add the tuna steak and cook for 3–4 minutes on each side – the steak should still be rare inside but seared on the outside. Slice into four portions and set aside.

Ladle the hummus broth into four shallow serving bowls, then arrange the tuna slices on top. Scatter with the capers, remaining coriander, eggs and olives if using. Serve immediately with griddled bread.

5

SHARE THE FEAST

LARGE PLATES AND PRINCIPAL DISHES

FLEXITARIAN ABUNDANCE

In a world of large family tribes, strong family ties and tight-knit communities, sharing of food is a necessity and a social ritual and feasting a natural reaping to break the fast. However, everyday feasting is not at all the same as celebratory feasts.

A Middle Eastern cook is the original flexitarian (perhaps!) having to be flexible in their cooking and draw inspiration from season, terroir and familial necessities. Meat is not always a suitable option – not only because of seasonality but also because of the sheer cost to feed a large family – and so cooking techniques have been established to cater to this. When meat is used, a little can go a long way! Meat can be stretched to feed a large family by sprinkling it into a stew along with some pulses and vegetables. Another way to make good use of very little meat is by combining it with burghul or rice as is the case with the never-ending array of kebbeh and keftah dishes of the Middle East. Large beast cooking is reserved for festive feasting, since meat becomes the focus and one of the ways to show how much one honours and values their guests. Rice or grain pilafs move from everyday to feast with ease. Ahead, I have shared dishes for everyday feasting as well as celebratory feasts.

FROM THE ISLAMIC AL HADITH

'FOOD FOR ONE IS ENOUGH FOR TWO, FOOD FOR TWO IS ENOUGH FOR FOUR, FOOD FOR FOUR IS ENOUGH FOR EIGHT!'

CHARRED ASPARAGUS & DRIED LIME SOUP

serves 4-6
prep 10 minutes
cook 25 minutes

750 g (1 lb 11 oz) asparagus
  spears, tough stalks
  trimmed and discarded
knob of Aged butter
  (page 27) or clarified butter
1 onion, finely chopped
5 garlic cloves, peeled and
  finely chopped
1 teaspoon pickled za'atar
  (page 82-83) or
  1 teaspoon dried thyme
1 dried lime, smashed
¼ teaspoon Aleppo pepper
  flakes or dried chilli flakes
60 ml (2 fl oz/¼ cup) arak
  or ouzo
flaky sea salt
1 litre (34 fl oz/4 cups)
  vegetable stock
3 tablespoons full-fat Greek
  yoghurt or labneh soft
  (page 25), to serve

Nowadays, asparagus is most often associated with European cuisine although its origins stretch back to the Mediterranean and South-west Asia, where the plant still grows wild. In the spring, we forage them near our home in Mount Lebanon and preserve them in brine, a fading tradition. Here, asparagus is charred and then combined with the unique taste of dried lime to produce an altogether lovely soup.

Preheat a grill (broiler) to high. Place the asparagus on a baking tray under the grill and cook for 4-5 minutes on each side until slightly charred at the edges. Remove and roughly chop.

Melt the butter in a saucepan over medium heat, add the onion and fry, stirring for 1-2 minutes. Reduce the heat, cover and sweat the onions over low heat for 4-5 minutes, until soft and translucent. Add the asparagus (reserving a few tips to garnish with later), garlic, pickled za'atar and dried lime, and cover and cook for a further minute. Add the Aleppo pepper flakes and arak and cook for a minute, then pour over the stock. Season with salt to taste, then bring to the boil over high heat. Once boiling, reduce the heat to low, cover and simmer for 10-15 minutes, or until the asparagus is completely tender.

Meanwhile, mix the labneh with 1 tablespoon of water, until slightly runny.

Once the soup has finished cooking, strain out the pieces of dried lime and use a hand blender to pulse the mixture to a fine purée. Add a little water or more broth if you prefer a thinner consistency. Divide between 4-6 serving bowls, pour over the yoghurt and then top with the reserved asparagus. Serve immediately.

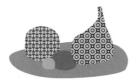

ROASTED GARLIC KISHKEEYA SOUP

serves   4–6
prep   10 minutes
cook   45 minutes

5 garlic heads, left unpeeled
1–2 tablespoons olive oil
2–3 tablespoons
   rapeseed oil
1 tablespoon butter
1 tablespoon dried mint
1 tablespoon finely
   chopped tarragon
125 g (4 oz/1 cup) kishk flour
   (page 98)
1 litre (34 fl oz/4 cups)
   vegetable stock or water
flaky sea salt and freshly
   ground black pepper
1 potato (400 g/14 oz),
   peeled and diced
100 g (3½ oz) Bacon
   basturma (page 95) or
   streaky bacon (optional),
   roughly chopped
250 g (9 oz) finely shredded
   cabbage or other seasonal
   leafy green vegetable
30 g (1 oz) ginger, peeled
   and finely chopped
Tempura onions (page 23),
   to garnish

A millennium-old hangover cure (fit for a millennial), kishk (page 100) was revered for its 'balanced properties' and used to make porridges known as kishkeeya in medieval Baghdad. Typically kishk soup is enjoyed for breakfast in the Levant and I can attest to its hangover zapping abilities and soul-soothing sorcery.

   Avoid grating or pressing the garlic, as anything that breaks down the garlic's cells will make the soup too pungent. Traditionally, the garlic is shaved into translucent slices and slow-cooked, but as we're often time poor (or just hungover) I have provided a passive approach, that is, baking the garlic until soft and unctuous. I prefer this method as it lends a sweetness to the resulting dish.

Preheat the oven to 200°C/400°F/Gas 6. Place the garlic heads on a large sheet of foil, drizzle with the olive oil, sprinkle with salt and pepper, toss to coat and seal well. Roast in the oven for 30–40 minutes, or until the garlic is caramelised and tender. Leave it to cool slightly. Carefully unwrap the foil and squeeze the garlic flesh out of the skins. Use the edge of a knife to purée the flesh and set aside, discarding any garlic skins.

Meanwhile, place a large frying pan over medium heat and add the rapeseed oil. Add the diced potato and fry for 6–7 minutes, until browned. Toss in the bacon basturma, if using, and cook for a further 2 minutes, then add the shredded cabbage and ginger, and stir to combine. Cook for a further 5 minutes, until the cabbage is soft. Season lightly with salt and pepper.

Place a large pan over low heat and melt the butter. Add the puréed garlic, mint and tarragon, and cook through for 1 minute. Stir in the kishk flour, along with the stock or water. Whisk together very well, increase the heat to high and bring to the boil. Reduce the heat to low and simmer for 10 minutes, slightly covered. Season lightly with salt and pepper – the kishk flour is already salty. Divide the kishk soup between 4–6 serving bowls, spoon over the cabbage and basturma topping and finally scatter with the onion tempura. Serve immediately.

YOGHURT, ALMOND & BARBERRY CHICKEN STEW

serves   4
prep   25 minutes
cook   1–2 hours

1 tablespoon clarified butter
1 kg (2 lb 3 oz) chicken legs,
   skin-on
1 onion, finely chopped
1 tablespoon Bezar spice mix
   (page 28)
1 small garlic head, peeled
   and very finely chopped
40 g (1½ oz/¼ cup) dried
   barberries or cranberries
85 g (3 oz/¾ cup) ground
   almonds
400 ml (13½ fl oz/1⅔ cups)
   chicken stock or water
1–2 bay leaves
300 g (10½ oz) green beans
300 g (10½ oz/1 heaped
   cup) full-fat Greek yoghurt
   (preferably goat's yoghurt)
handful mint, finely
   chopped, to garnish
2–3 tablespoons lightly
   toasted almonds,
   to garnish
flaky sea salt and freshly
   ground black pepper

This stew comes in varying names depending on whether its made with lamb shank or chicken. There is a pinch of myth going on in recipes about cooking with yoghurt to avoid curdling. While it is true that adding starch to help absorb the water, and yolk emulsifiers to help prevent the casein proteins from gathering together into noticeable curds are effective ways of stabilising yoghurt, stirring in only one direction is not! What *is* crucial is stirring often, in any direction, as is using a full-fat yoghurt. Curdling occurs when a protein does not have enough fat molecules to bind to and thus appearance of separation or curdling becomes very pronounced. In light of this, I suggest the use of a full-fat, strained yoghurt. By following the method below and adding the yoghurt towards the end of cooking, you will have a curdle-free stew without needing to use a stabilising agent.

Place a heavy-based pan with a lid over medium heat and melt half of the butter. Season the chicken legs and add, skin side down, to the pan. Brown the skin all over for 2–3 minutes, avoid moving them around so as not to tear the skin. Cover the pan with the lid and reduce the heat to low. Cook for about 1 minute, then remove the lid and, using a spatula, gently turn over the chicken. Increase the heat to high and cook, uncovered, for a further 2–3 minutes. Transfer the chicken to a plate.

Add the remaining butter to the pan, reduce the heat to medium-low, then add the onion and spice mix. Toss well and cook for 4–5 minutes, or until the onion is soft and translucent. Next, add the garlic and barberries, and cook for a further minute. Add the ground almonds, toss, then add the stock and bay leaves. Increase the heat to high, cover and bring to the boil. Reduce the heat to low and slow-cook for 1–2 hours, or until the meat is cooked through and tender. The broth should be slightly thickened.

Meanwhile, bring a saucepan of water to the boil and blanch the green beans for 3–4 minutes, until just tender. Remove from the heat, drain and refresh under cold water. Set aside.

Once the chicken is cooked, remove it and set aside on a plate. Take the pan off the heat and slowly whisk in the yoghurt. Add the green beans and return the pan to the heat. Cover and simmer very gently over low heat for about 10 minutes, ensuring the sauce does not come to the boil. Season with salt and pepper to taste and serve immediately, sprinkled with freshly chopped mint and lightly toasted almonds.

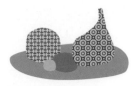

OX CHEEK, SHALLOT & RHUBARB STEW

serves 4–6
prep 10 minutes
cook 2–2½ hours

20 g (¾ oz) butter
200 g (7 oz) (about 12 shallots), peeled and whole
700 g (1 lb 9 oz) ox cheek, sliced into 4 chunks
20 g (¾ oz) ginger, peeled and finely chopped
½ nutmeg, grated
1 tablespoon ground turmeric
5 smoked garlic cloves, peeled and crushed
handful finely chopped parsley
flaky sea salt and freshly ground black pepper
handful finely chopped mint
200 g (7 oz) rhubarb, cut into 2.5 cm (1 in) diagonal chunks
Caliph's scorched rice (page 217), to serve

In the West, rhubarb tends to be restricted to a sweet context, and not much beyond rhubarb crumble and cocktail spritzers. While I enjoy both, my favourite use of rhubarb is in savoury stews such as here. Used in Iranian cooking to thicken and sour stews since ancient times, it is also celebrated for its health benefits as is believed to cleanse the body. Light and comforting, I enjoy this stew with the Persian rice or Loaded grains on page 219.

Melt the butter in a large saucepan over medium heat. Add the shallots, tossing to cover with the butter and frying for 5–8 minutes, until browned. Remove using a slotted spoon and transfer to a plate. Set aside.

Add the ox cheek to the pan and brown on each side for 1–2 minutes. Add the ginger, nutmeg, turmeric and garlic, and cook for a further minute, stirring at all times. Pour in 750 ml (25½ fl oz/3 cups) water and season with salt and pepper. Simmer over low heat, covered, for 1½ hours – the liquid should have thickened. If not, simmer uncovered for a further 30 minutes until the meat is meltingly tender, making sure to occasionally cover the meat with any juices if their peaks are poking through the juice.

Finally, add the herbs, rhubarb and the seared shallots and cook for a further 10 minutes over the lowest heat. Remove from the heat and leave the stew to sit for 10 minutes. Taste and adjust the seasoning to taste, adding more salt or pepper as preferred, and serve with rice.

PORK KEFTEDES

IN AVGOLEMONO SAUCE WITH CRISPY VERMICELLI

serves 4
prep 20 minutes
cook 15–20 minutes

for the keftedes:
1 onion, quartered
handful parsley
3 garlic cloves, peeled
450 g (1 lb) minced (ground)
  pork, beef or lamb
1 teaspoon ground allspice
2 teaspoons flaky sea salt,
  plus extra to taste
25 g (1 oz) cashews, toasted

155 g (5½ oz/1 cup) shelled
  green peas
generous knob of butter
100 g (3½ oz) short
  vermicelli (available from
  Middle Eastern grocers)
1 litre (34 fl oz/4 cups) beef
  stock
4 eggs
zest and juice of 1 lemon
few basil leaves (preferably
  Greek), to serve

Keftedes is plural for *kefte*, the Greek word for kefta. Essentially aromatic meatballs enrobed in a silky *avgolemono* sauce (egg- and lemon-based sauce), it is a pure comfort dish for me. The meatballs in the sauce remind me of the kebbehs in yoghurt and the kafta in tahini that I've grown so accustomed to. This is indulgent, homely but gorgeous. Ideally, ask your butcher to mince (grind) the pork two or three times to make it ultra-tender. Otherwise, a food processor works just as well.

Blitz the onion in a food processor once or twice. Scrape down the sides then add the parsley and garlic and blitz a few more times to produce a rough purée-like consistency (don't overdo it otherwise the mixture will be too wet). Add the mince, allspice and salt, then blitz for a further 1–2 minutes, stopping to scrape down the sides a few times and making sure all the ingredients are incorporated evenly. Pinch off a tiny piece of the mixture and quickly fry in a small saucepan with a little oil. Taste and adjust the seasoning. Avoid adding too much salt – the seasoning will intensify as the mixture sits in the fridge.

Form the mixture into small golf ball-sized meatballs, carving out a shallow hole in centre of each meatball and then pressing a cashew in. Use more mixture to seal and cover the cashew, making sure the cashew is not protruding from the sides. Transfer the meatballs to a plate as you go. The mixture should yield about 20 meatballs. Cover with cling film (plastic wrap) and transfer to the fridge to sit while you finish the rest of the dish. These can be prepared a day ahead or made and frozen.

Meanwhile, place the peas in a small bowl, cover with boiling water, cover with a plate and set aside for at least 10 minutes or until just cooked.

To make the crispy vermicelli, melt the butter in a small frying pan over medium heat. When foaming, add the vermicelli and fry for 2 minutes, or until golden and crisp. Remove with a slotted spoon and drain on kitchen towel.

Place the stock in a saucepan over medium heat and bring to the boil. Reduce the heat to low, add the meatballs and gently simmer for 2 minutes, or until the meatballs have cooked through. Use a slotted spoon to remove and transfer to a plate. Set aside somewhere warm. Take the pan of stock off the heat.

Beat the eggs, lemon zest and juice in a jug. Measure out 120 ml (4 fl oz/½ cup) of the stock and gradually pour into the egg mixture, whisking constantly. Pour this mixture slowly into the pan with the remaining stock, whisking rigorously. Place back over very low heat and stir constantly for a couple of minutes until creamy – it should be thick enough to coat the back of a wooden spoon. Remove from the heat and carefully stir in the meatballs and peas. Season to taste. Serve immediately in individual bowls, with crispy vermicelli and basil sprinkled over.

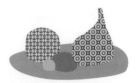

SMOKED COD TAJEN

WITH CLEMENTINE & BRONZED ONION TAHINI

serves   4
prep   15 minutes
cook   15 minutes

80 ml (2½ fl oz/⅓ cup) olive
   oil
2 onions, thinly sliced
1 garlic head, peeled and
   finely chopped
1 tablespoon ground
   turmeric
1 tablespoon ground cumin
1 tablespoon ground ginger
½ tablespoon ground black
   pepper
½ teaspoon white pepper
½ tablespoon dried tarragon
250 ml (8½ fl oz/1 cup) tahini
juice of 1 grapefruit
juice of 1 lemon
1–2 clementines or 1 orange,
   peeled and roughly
   chopped
240 ml (8 fl oz/scant 1 cup)
   white wine
flaky sea salt and freshly
   ground black pepper
750 g (1 lb 11 oz) lightly
   smoked cod, haddock
   or halibut fillets
2 tablespoons flaked
   almonds, lightly toasted
2 tablespoons pine nuts,
   lightly toasted
fresh tarragon or coriander
   (cilantro), finely chopped,
   to serve
lemon wedges, to serve

The *tajen* here is the name of the shallow pan used to traditionally prepare the dish. I like to use a shallow baking dish that I can transfer directly to the table to serve.

Preheat the oven to 180°C/350°F/Gas 4. Grease an ovenproof dish with 2 tablespoons of the oil.

Place a frying pan over medium-high heat, add the remaining oil and cook the onions for 4–5 minutes, until lightly browned. Add the garlic, spices and dried tarragon, reduce the heat to medium-low, cover and cook for a further 2–3 minutes.

Meanwhile, whisk together the tahini, grapefruit and lemon juices with about 250 ml (8½ fl oz/1 cup) water. You want the mixture to be a thick and pourable consistency, but not runny.

Once the onions have sweated down, add the clementines, increase the heat to high and let them brown along the edges for about a minute. Pour over the wine, and allow to simmer and evaporate for about 1–2 minutes. Season with salt and pepper. Whisk in the tahini mixture and cook for a further 2–3 minutes until the mixture has thickened and looks like it will nicely enrobe the fish. Set aside.

Arrange the cod fillets in the greased dish and season with salt and pepper, then roast for 10–12 minutes or until cooked through and opaque. Pour the warm tahini sauce over the fish and grill (broil) on high for another 2–3 minutes. Sprinkle with the toasted almonds, pine nuts and fresh tarragon or coriander. Serve immediately with lemon wedges on the side.

IN A TWIST OVER MUSAQA'A

Today, moussaka (Arabic *musaqa'a* meaning 'cold') is a traditional dish in the Levant, Middle East and Balkans, with local and regional variations and a kitchen sink of nomenclatures.

In most of the Levant and in particular Syria and Lebanon, musaqa'a, as we call it in my family, is also known as *maghmour* (page 144) – it's medieval precursor name. The names, and there's no doubt there are others, are not defined by borders, which makes any tracing of the dish's history all the more perplexing. However, it's obvious that aside from aubergines (eggplants) and tomatoes the Levantine musaqa'a is a delicious cold, vegetarian brew, loyal to its name, so it must have arisen here. Or did it? The Iraqis have a meat version which they also call *tebsi* – denoting 'tray' – as it's served straight from the baking tray, hot out of the oven. The plot thickens when we enter the kitchens of the Balkans: Turkey, Greece, Serbia, Bulgaria, etc. All use minced (ground) meat and the now-omnipresent layered, oven-baked Greek moussaka sees a French béchamel, too. The Slavic мусака (*musaka*) takes a whole other twist with potato and egg custard. In any case, the Balkan moussakas are not served cold, so the Arabic word musaqa'a is misused. Or not. I have another theory on the origin of the word. Could it be purely coincidence that in borrowing the dish from the Turks, the word sounded like 'cold' in Arabic, and so just stuck? Was it perhaps borrowed by the Turks first from a different Arabic term *moussaqa* meaning 'watered' (implying 'with sauce') and then mistakingly re-adapted by the Arabs as musaqa'a because they served it cold?

Nawal Nasrallah first theorised that too, but her paper, *In the beginning there was no musaqa'a* further states that it could be 'derived from the verb *saqa'a*, one of the meanings of which is "spread flat"'.

The reality is that cuisine is ever evolving and musaqa'a, like many other historical dishes, has a twisted past. As Bernard Lewis so brilliantly puts it 'etymology can be either misleading or instructive'.

For now, I'll offer you my own twisted moussaka, somewhat Greek-inspired using my kishkamel, page 205.

KISHKAMEL MOUSSAKA

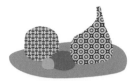

serves 6-8
prep 30 minutes
cook 1 hour

1.5 kg (3lb 5 oz) aubergines
 (eggplants), thinly sliced
60 ml (2 fl oz/¼ cup) olive
 oil
5-6 tomatoes, or 400 g
 (14 oz) passata
generous knob of butter
1 large onion, finely chopped
450 g (1 lb) minced (ground)
 lamb
1 teaspoon ground allspice
½ teaspoon salt
½ teaspoon ground white
 pepper
2 tablespoons tomato paste
450 g (1 lb) mix of halloumi
 and Cheddar, shredded
green salad leaves, to serve

for the kishkamel:
40 g (1½ oz) butter
1 garlic head, cloves peeled
 and very finely chopped
125 g (4 oz/1 cup) kishk flour
 (page 101)
flaky sea salt

Kishk is a hugely versatile ingredient and one I like to put to use in surprising ways, such as in the fermented béchamel used here, or as my friend Hisham coined it, 'kishkamel'. Everyone that has tasted this dish, including kishk virgins and kishk haters, have ended up loving it.

Preheat the oven to 200°C/400°F/Gas 6. Brush the aubergines with the oil and arrange them in a single layer on a baking tray. Roast for 10-15 minutes, or until cooked through. Set aside and leave the oven on.

Meanwhile, make the kishkamel. Melt the butter in a small saucepan over medium-low heat, add the garlic and fry for 1-2 minutes. Lower the heat and add the kishk flour, stir to combine, then pour in 500 ml (17 fl oz/ 2 cups) water, whisking to form a homogenous mixture. Increase the heat and bring to the boil, season with salt to taste, reduce the heat, cover and simmer for 10-15 minutes until thickened (you're after the consistency of thick but pourable cream). If you need to thin out the sauce, gradually add more warm water.

If using fresh tomatoes, make a cross incision at the base of the tomatoes and place in a bowl. Pour over boiling water. Leave to sit for 5 minutes, then peel, de-seed and chop the flesh. Set aside.

Add the butter to a pan over medium-low heat, add the onion, cover and sweat for 7-10 minutes, until soft and translucent. Stir often. Increase the heat to high, add the minced meat, allspice, salt and pepper, and brown the meat, breaking it up with a wooden spoon. This should take about 5 minutes. Next, add the chopped tomatoes and tomato paste, then stir to combine. Cover and simmer to reduce for about 15 minutes.

Layer half of the aubergine slices in the bottom of a baking dish in an overlapping manner. Spread over the meat mixture, followed by the remaining aubergine slices, overlapping them again. Drizzle over the sauce and sprinkle with cheese. Bake in the oven for 30-40 minutes, until the mixture is bubbling and thickened. Place under a hot grill (broiler) for 3-5 minutes to brown the top if necessary. Serve hot with fresh green salad leaves.

TO STUFF OR BE STUFFED

Several countries bordering or in the Caucasus are wrapped up in a long-running gastro-war over the origin and ownership of the stuffed leaf and vegetable culinary heritage.

The practice of wrapping stuffings in vine, cabbage or fig leaves, and then slow-cooking them in a flavoured broth, is believed to go as far back as the third millennium BC to the ancient Mesopotamian empires. More 'recently', with the help of invading Muslims in the 11th century, the art of stuffing spread, reaching its pinnacle in the elaborate banquets of Ottoman palace kitchens. *Dolma*, plural *dolmades* – considered to be an inflection of the Turkish verb *dolmak*, meaning 'to be stuffed' – is the word used most consistently within the region for this family of dishes. The Armenians, whose version is called *tolma,* claim their etymology goes deeper: *toli* and *ma* mean 'vine leaf' and 'wrapped' respectively. The use of toli as a grape leaf is recorded much earlier than Ottoman times, in the inscriptions of the Kingdom of Van in the ninth to sixth centuries BC). But, to say they belong to a certain country is ludicrous in my opinion.

There is an incessant compulsion to stuff everything here. Fruits, beasts and their derivatives (intestines and sausages) are stuffed and characteristic of the region's cuisine. Traditionally, the upper classes stuffed whole lambs while the lower classes used vegetables or whatever else they could afford. All manner of edible leaves may be stuffed – cooked or uncooked – grape, cabbage, Swiss chard, monk's rhubarb, strawberry and raspberry. Fruits such as quince, pumpkin and tomatoes make for wonderful edible chariots. Most, if not all, vegetables are stuffed too – if you can core it, you can stuff it.

Stuffings are typically minced (ground) and seasoned beef or lamb, sometimes pork and fish, together with grains, pulses or a combination thereof, varying according to season and terroir. Some dolmades are seasoned with mint, dill, parsley and coriander. Others simply call on cinnamon or allspice. The addition of dried fruits and nuts, such as raisins, currants and pine nuts, is popular. Herby tabbouleh leftovers, bulked up with cracked chickpeas (garbanzo beans), more burghul and pine nuts, make for a great stuffing and another ingenious example of food recycling in the region. The use of sliced onions, tomatoes, lemons, potatoes, ribs or chops and garlic to layer the pot is also a popular technique and makes for a delicious main, see page 118. Meat dolmades are generally served warm, typically accompanied by a sauce. Meatless ones are served ideally at room temperature.

FREEKEH-STUFFED ONION

IN FETA & VERJUICE SAUCE

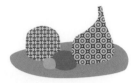

serves 6–8
prep 20 minutes
cook 1–1½ hours

2 tablespoons olive oil,
    plus extra to grease
1.5 kg (3 lb 5 oz) mixture
    white and red onions
    (6–8 smaller ones or
    4 large ones)
knob of butter
80 g (2¾ oz) sujuk or
    chorizo, cubed
½ teaspoon smoked paprika
1 teaspoon Aleppo pepper
    flakes or dried chilli flakes
1 tomato, chopped
1 garlic clove, peeled and
    finely chopped
80 g (2¾ oz/½ cup) cracked
    freekeh
3 tablespoons finely
    chopped parsley
flaky sea salt
240 ml (8 fl oz/scant 1 cup)
    vegetable stock
2 tablespoons verjuice or
    cider vinegar
75 g (2¾ oz) feta, crumbled,
    plus more to garnish
2–3 tablespoons pine nuts,
    toasted, to serve

In the Middle East, onions are often peeled, and the peels or layers stuffed and rolled like vine leaves. However, this is an equally lovely alternative.

Preheat the oven to 200°C/400°F/Gas 6. Lightly grease a baking dish with oil.

Prepare the onions. Cut a 1.5 cm (½ in) thick slice from the top of the onions, reserving the caps. If required, shave enough from the bottoms so that the onions can stand upright. Using a corer or a small spoon, carefully scoop out all but the 2 outer layers, being careful not to pierce the onions. Reserve the scooped-out onion flesh and finely chop. Transfer the hollowed onions and their caps to the prepared dish, rub all over with a little of the oil, cover with foil and bake in the oven for about 20 minutes while you prep the stuffing.

Place a frying pan over medium-low heat, melt the butter, then add the chopped onions and cook for 3–4 minutes, until softened. Add the sujuk, paprika, Aleppo pepper flakes, tomato and garlic, and cook for a few minutes until the onions are translucent. Add the freekeh, toss to combine and cover with 160 ml (5½ fl oz/generous ½ cup) water. Increase the heat to high, bring to the boil, reduce the heat to low and simmer, covered, for 10–15 minutes or until the freekeh has cooked through. (It's fine if the freekeh is al dente or slightly wet – it will continue to cook in the oven.) Add the parsley and season to taste with salt.

Remove the baked onions from the oven. Divide the onion and freekeh mixture evenly between the cavities of the onions – don't worry if the filling overflows a little. Arrange the caps on top, pour over the stock and verjuice and cover with foil. Return to the oven to cook for 45 minutes, or until the onions are tender yet still have a bit of bite.

Remove the foil and onion caps and place under a preheated grill (broiler) to char for 5 minutes. Use a slotted spoon to transfer the stuffed onions to individual dishes or a large serving platter. Add the feta to the juices in the dish and whisk until smooth. Drizzle this sauce over the onions and sprinkle with extra feta and pine nuts. Serve immediately.

MAFTOUL-STUFFED TURNIP

AND KOHLRABI IN BEETROOT BROTH

serves 6–8
prep 1 hour
cook 1 hour

800 g (1 lb 2 oz) turnips
800 g (1 lb 2 oz) kohlrabi

for the stuffing:
2 tablespoons olive oil
1 onion, finely chopped
1 teaspoon caraway seeds
5 garlic cloves, peeled
  and crushed
1 teaspoon ground allspice
½ teaspoon ground cinnamon
2 teaspoons ground cumin
1 tablespoon paprika
1 teaspoon ground turmeric
100 g (3½ oz) kohlrabi
  greens (with stalks, if any)
  or 1 leek, finely chopped
140 g (5 oz) watercress,
  finely chopped
75 g (2¾ oz) cooked
  chickpeas (garbanzo
  beans) (page 72) or tinned
  chickpeas, drained and rinsed
125 g (4 oz) Palestinian
  maftoul or moghrabieh
  (pearl couscous)
100 g (3½ oz) walnuts, toasted
zest of 1 orange
flaky sea salt and freshly
  ground black pepper

for the beetroot broth:
2 tablespoons olive oil
3 small beetroot (beets), with
  stalks if any, finely chopped
1 teaspoon ground cumin
½ teaspoon caraway seeds
3 garlic cloves, peeled and
  finely chopped
2 anchovies, tinned in oil
  optional
340 ml (11½ fl oz/1⅓ cups)
  cider or pale ale
750 ml (25½ fl oz/3 cups)
  vegetable stock or water
juice of 1 orange
1 tablespoon finely chopped
  dill
full-fat Greek yoghurt, to serve

This recipe is inspired by one of the oldest cookbooks in the world, an Akkadian clay tablet highlighting recipes from Babylon, circa 1700 BC. Beetroot and beer (or in this case, cider) were comrades of their time and their influence can still be seen in the Jewish-Iraqi kubba in beetroot sauce. Here, moghrabieh (pearl couscous) can be a substitute for the earthy Palestinian maftoul.

Slice the tops off each of the turnips and the kohlrabi. Use a corer or a spoon to carve out the middles, leaving about a 5 mm (¼ in) thickness. Reserve the innards, placing them in a bowl, cover and set aside in the fridge. You can use the reserved innards in the kuku on page 129.

Make the stuffing. Heat the oil in a saucepan over high heat. Add the onion and caraway seeds, reduce the heat to medium, cover and sweat for 2–3 minutes. Add the garlic, spices, kohlrabi greens, watercress and cook, uncovered, for 2–3 minutes, until aromatic and the greens have wilted. Remove from the heat, add in the chickpeas, maftoul, walnuts, grated orange zest and toss to combine. Season to taste with salt and pepper. Set aside.

Preheat the oven to 200°C/400°F/Gas 6.

Add 2 tablespoons oil to a heavy-based, ovenproof pan and place over medium heat. Add the beetroot, cumin and caraway, toss to combine and cook for 1–2 minutes, until aromatic. Add the garlic and, if using, toss in the anchovies and cook for a further minute. Pour over the cider and cook for 1–2 minutes. Pour over the stock, orange juice and finely chopped dill, stir to combine and season with salt to taste. Bring the mixture to the boil over high heat, then cover and simmer over low heat for 10–15 minutes or until the beetroot has softened and cooked through.

Meanwhile, spoon the stuffing mixture into the hollowed out vegetables. Set aside.

Once the beetroot has softened and cooked through, use a hand blender to blitz to a purée. Carefully transfer the stuffed vegetables to the pan with the beetroot purée, standing them up and placing the reserved caps on top accordingly. Cover and bake in the oven for 40–50 minutes, or until the vegetables are tender and cooked through. Serve immediately with yoghurt on the side.

JAZAR MEHSHE

VENISON-STUFFED CARROTS

WITH MINTED PEA MUTABAL

serves 4–6
prep 45 minutes
cook 30 minutes

1.4 kg (3 lb 1 oz) or 4 very
 large carrots of roughly
 equal size
2 tablespoons olive oil
2 tablespoons tamarind
 paste
2 tablespoons tomato paste
sea salt and freshly ground
 black pepper

for the stuffing:
175 g (6 oz) minced
 (ground) venison
½ celery stalk, very finely
 chopped
½ onion, very finely
 chopped
2 garlic cloves, peeled and
 crushed
½ teaspoon ground allspice
½ teaspoon ground ginger
¼ teaspoon ground white
 pepper
¼ teaspoon ground nutmeg
40 g (1½ oz) cooked
 chestnuts, roughly
 chopped
honey, to taste (optional)

for the minted pea mutabal:
1 tablespoon butter
500 g (1 lb 2 oz) peas
2 tablespoons full-fat
 plain yoghurt
1 tablespoon finely
 chopped mint

This is best made in the autumn months when you can find large
purple carrots. You could also mix in some parsnips. It's a labour of
love, especially if cored traditionally, and the carrot is kept whole.
I find slicing it in wedges a less frustrating alternative, yet still offering
up a quirky meal. We have a special, long coring tool in the Middle
East which can be found at Middle Eastern grocers.

Fill a large pan with 1 litre (34 fl oz/4 cups) water over a high heat, add
a little salt, cover and bring to the boil.

Meanwhile, trim the carrots into 2.5 cm (1 in) wedges, using the first
carrot cut as a template. Blanch the carrots in the boiling water for
2–3 minutes, or until slightly softened – you do not want cooked carrots.
Drain, reserving 750 ml (25½ fl oz/3 cups) water. Rinse the carrots under
cold water to stop them cooking.

Using a long vegetable corer or long, sharp, thin knife blade, carefully core
out the innards of the carrots, making sure not to puncture the carrot or
hurt yourself. (All is not lost if you puncture a carrot though.) You want
to end up with a round of carrot you can see through like a tunnel. Make
sure the edges are cored evenly and as thinly as possible.

Make the stuffing. Combine the minced meat, celery, onion, garlic, spices,
chestnuts, and honey, if using. Season with salt and mix well. Using two
fingers, and the corer, if available, stuff the cavity of the carrots with the
meat filling, pushing it through to fill completely. If you've punctured the
carrots, let some of the meat escape and apply pressure on the area as
you continue to fill the cavity to seal (this will prevent the stuffing from
bursting out when cooking). Shape any excess filling into small meatballs
and cook alongside the carrots as 'chef's privilege' nibbles.

Return the pan used to boil the carrots to medium heat. Add the oil
and fry the carrots on each side for 1–2 minutes, or until golden.

Dissolve the tamarind and tomato paste in the reserved carrot cooking
water and pour into the pan. Bring to the boil, reduce the heat and
simmer for about 30 minutes, or until the stuffing is cooked through and
the carrots are tender yet still al dente.

Meanwhile, make the mutabal. Place a saucepan over medium-high and
melt the butter. Add the peas and cook, stirring often, until warmed
through, about 5 minutes. Add the yoghurt and use a hand blender to blitz
the mixture to the desired consistency. Stir in the mint and season with
salt and pepper. Serve the stuffed carrots warm with the pea mutabal
dolloped on the side.

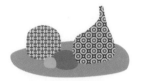

LOQUAT KEBBEH

WITH ZA'ATAR & SUMAC

serves   6–8
prep   20 minutes
cook   45 minutes

1 onion, roughly chopped
300 g (10½ oz) fine burghul,
   rinsed and drained
½ teaspoon ground white
   pepper
½ teaspoon ground allspice
¼ teaspoon ground
   cinnamon
1 tablespoon ground cumin
2 tablespoons dried
   marjoram
2 tablespoons dried za'atar
   or dried oregano
500 g (1 lb 2 oz) minced
   (ground) lamb
3 tablespoons olive oil, plus
   60 ml (2 fl oz) for greasing
Cucumber and mint yoghurt
   (page 81), to serve

I really thought nothing could compare with the traditional lamb kebbeh pie; what we call *kebbeh bel sayneeyeh* or 'kebbeh in a baking tray'. This version, however, takes it to another dimension and I assure you I'm not being biased. I add whatever seasonal fruit I have on hand – apple, nectarines and cherries – all of which have been hits amongst kebbeh connoisseurs. The recipe might appear lengthy, but, once you've made this a few times, you'll be ready to do it blindfolded.

In a small food processor, blitz the onion to a fine paste. Remove and strain, keeping the juices and the onion purée separate.

Add the burghul to a large bowl and use your hands to rub in the reserved onion juices. Stir in the spices and season, then pour over 275 ml (9½ fl oz/1 cup) water. Use a fork to fluff and set aside for about 10 minutes.

Preheat the oven to 200°C/400°F/Gas 6.

Meanwhile, make the filling. Melt the butter in a frying pan and sauté the pine nuts for about 1 minute or just until starting to colour, then add the red onion for 1–2 minutes until softened. Add the loquats, Aleppo pepper flakes, mint and sumac. Season, stir well and set aside.

The burghul should have absorbed all of the water. If not, squeeze out the excess water very well. Taste and adjust the seasoning. Add the lamb and puréed onion, and mix well. Transfer the mixture to the food processor, in batches, pulsing it to produce a fine paste. Stop once the mixture has become a cohesive paste. This process should take 2–3 minutes. Pinch off a small piece and quickly fry it in a small frying pan until cooked. Taste. Adjust the seasoning of the mixture to your preference.

for the loquat filling:
knob of butter
handful pine nuts
1 red onion, thinly sliced
150 g (5½ oz) loquats,
 thinly sliced
1 teaspoon Aleppo pepper
 flakes or dried chilli flakes
1 tablespoon dried mint
1 tablespoon ground sumac
flaky sea salt and freshly
 ground black pepper

To a small bowl, add some water and ice cubes. Grease a 23 cm (9 in) round dish or baking tin with oil. Spread a third of the meat paste out onto the base of the greased dish, creating a thin, even layer. Dip your fingers into the bowl of iced water to help make it easier to spread.

Next, tip the loquat filling on top of the layer of meat and spread evenly. Roll out the remaining meat mixture between two sheets of baking paper (parchment) to the circumference of your dish or tin. Remove the top layer of paper, then using the bottom paper layer, transfer the rolled out dough by gently flipping this layer over the filling in the dish. Then dab your fingers in the iced water and very gently stretch the meat to connect it together, creating an even top layer.

Using a knife, gently cut the pie into quarters, and then repeat once more to create *eight* triangular slices. Score the top layer of each triangle diagonally and then across again to create diamond shapes. Using your thumb, create a small hole in the centre where the triangular points all meet, then create baseless pyramids in the centre of each triangle, making sure they continue along the same line, to achieve a star pattern. Drizzle over the oil and bake in the oven for 40 minutes, until golden brown on top. Serve with cucumber and mint yoghurt.

PARBOILED RICE

serves   8
prep   30–35 minutes
cook   45 minutes

500 g (17½ oz/4 cups)
   basmati rice
4 tablespoons sea salt

'Good living is with rice, let the burghul hang itself.' Rice, as we might surmise from this quote, is in fact not considered a staple but rather a luxury. While evidence of the exact birthplace of this wild grass is a little muddied, we do know that it was cultivated along the periphery of the burghul crescent of the Levant in ancient times. This cultivation was scarce, however, in comparison to burghul. It was a prestigious grain, reserved for puddings, porridges and bread.

Following a steamy encounter between the Mughal (Indian) and Safavid (Persian/Iranian) empires around the mid-17th century, rice began to puff up on more occasions in the region's pots. Today, we notice this influence in the various dishes known under corruptions of the word 'pilaf', which ultimately descends from an Indian origin. An Iraqi folk song asks, 'O people of heaven, O people of hell, what do you eat?' The people in heaven turn out to live on rice and apricots, while the people in hell eat bulgur and tomatoes. I'm neither going to hang the rice nor the burghul and certainly not the freekeh. So I've offered a variety of rice recipes ahead as well as my Loaded grains recipe (page 219) for the people of hell, the people of heaven or just mere mortals.

Use this recipe to make the Tahdeeg rice two ways, large or small (see opposite and page 218), as well as the Candied beetroot maqluba (page 224). You can parboil the rice the day before and store it in the fridge, but bring it back to room temperature before using.

Remove any dirt or discoloured grains. Rinse the rice several times, under running water, until it runs clear. Add the rice to a large bowl, cover with water and add 2 tablespoons of the salt and leave to soak for 30 minutes. Strain the rice and rinse under tepid water.

Fill a large saucepan two-thirds with water and add the remaining 2 tablespoons of salt. Bring to the boil over high heat and stir. Once the water reaches a rolling boil, add the rice. Cook, uncovered, for 3 minutes over high heat until the rice is softened but still firm in the centre. Drain the rice and rinse well under cold running water. Set aside for about 10 minutes to strain well.

TAHDEEG RICE TWO WAYS

The crispy, scorched crust that develops while steaming rice is known as *hikake* in Iraq and *tahdeeq* in Iran and is the crown-jewel of any table.

CALIPHS' SCORCHED RICE

¼ teaspoon saffron threads

3-6 tablespoons rapeseed oil

1 x quantity parboiled rice, opposite

55 g (2 oz) butter, melted

In a small bowl, stir the saffron threads with 3 tablespoons of warm water. Heat the oil in a heavy-based and wide, non-stick saucepan over medium heat, pour in the saffron water. Sprinkle 4-5 tablespoons parboiled rice across the base of the pan to start with and then continue sprinkling over the remaining rice, making sure the whole base is covered and that the layers are even. Use the handle of a wooden spoon to make three holes in the rice to the bottom of the pan. Pour over the melted butter.

Wrap the lid of the pan in a clean kitchen towel and tie it into a tight knot at the handle, then cover the pan with the lid (the kitchen towel will prevent the moisture from dripping into the rice and making it soggy). Reduce the heat to low and cook, covered, for a further 20–40 minutes. The timing will depend on whether you prefer the rice golden and quite loose grained or formed in shape and a darker caramel colour.

When the rice is cooked, fill your kitchen basin with cold water to come up to about 5 cm (2 in). Remove the pan from the heat, place the base into the cold water and leave to sit for 1-2 minutes. This step helps to shock the rice and loosen the tahdeeg. Remove the lid and carefully invert the tardeeg onto a serving plate. Use a wooden spoon to tap the base of the pan to help it come away. Alternatively, you can spoon the rice out and break up the tahdeeg for serving.

EMPRESS' (RICE) LOVE CAKES

1 cup labneh or strained
    Greek yoghurt (page 25)
2 egg yolks
1 x quantity parboiled rice
    (page 216)
flaky sea salt
1-2 tablespoons rapeseed oil
celery leaves, rose petals,
    vine leaves, barberries
    (optional)
1-2 loaves of Arabic bread
33 x 7¾ cm (13 x 3 in) muffin
    tin pan

Preheat the oven to 175°C/350°F/Gas 4

Combine the labneh or yoghurt and egg yolks together, then add in the parboiled rice. Season with salt, if needed. Lightly grease a muffin tin and then add the flower or herb in each cavity. Spoon the yoghurt rice into each cavity evenly. You should make about 8 cakes. Cover with a loaf of Arabic bread (this mimics the tea towel effect on the previous page) and then seal very well with foil.

Bake in the oven for about 30-40 minutes, until crisp and golden. Remove from the oven and leave to rest for a minute or two. Remove the foil and crisp bread (perfectly crisp and still edible) and then lay a large enough baking sheet over the the muffin tin and flip it over. Use a spatula to get any stubborn cupcakes, being careful not to break them apart. If you find they need further crisping, then grill them on high for a minute or two but watch out they don't burn. See photo on pages 162-163.

LOADED GRAINS

serves 4–6
prep 15 minutes
cook 30 minutes

85 g (3 oz) butter
3 tablespoons pine nuts
3 tablespoons sliced
  almonds
3 tablespoons halved
  cashews
3 tablespoons pistachios
1 onion, finely chopped
1 celery stalk, finely chopped
450 g (1 lb) minced
  (ground) lamb
1 tablespoon ground sumac
½ teaspoon ground ginger
½ teaspoon mustard seeds
½ teaspoon ground allspice
¼ teaspoon ground
  cinnamon
¼ teaspoon ground nutmeg
¼ teaspoon ground
  cardamom
¼ teaspoon ground white
  pepper
⅛ teaspoon cracked black
  pepper
⅛ teaspoon ground cloves
1 tablespoon flaky sea salt
6 garlic cloves, peeled and
  finely chopped
3 tablespoons dried
  barberries
175 g (6 oz/1 cup) cracked
  freekeh, rinsed in water
  and drained
190 g (6½ oz/½ cup) basmati
  rice, rinsed in water and
  drained
115 g (4 oz/½ cup) coarse
  (grade 4) burghul, rinsed
  in water and drained
  (see page 15 for further
  clarification)
zest of ½ small orange
1 carrot, grated

Hashweh means stuffing and this is my multigrain riff on the typical stuffing in the Middle East. It can also be used as a main or a side in itself. I am using all three grains traditionally found in a hashweh. Try it stuffed into the cavity of a roast chicken, or it's equally as good as a side to lamb. It makes a wonderful quick lunch option with a dollop of yoghurt.

Place a frying pan over medium heat. Melt the butter, add the pine nuts and lightly brown, remove using a slotted spoon and set aside on a paper-towel-lined plate. Repeat with the almonds, cashews and pistachios (though these just require a minute to release their oils).

Add the onion and celery to the pan, and stir to coat with the remaining butter and cook over medium-low heat for 4–5 minutes, until soft and slightly browned. Toss in the minced lamb, all the spices and the salt, then mix to combine. Cook for 4–5 minutes, until browned, then add the garlic and barberries and cook for a further minute until aromatic. Toss in the grains, cover with about 750 ml (25½ fl oz/3 cups) water and bring to the boil over high heat. Reduce the heat, cover and simmer for about 10 minutes. Add the orange zest and carrot but don't stir. Continue to cook for a further 10 minutes, or until the water has been absorbed by the grains. Use a fork to give everything a final stir and transfer to a serving bowl and serve.

Also try: For a vegetarian option, substitute the lamb for cooked brown lentils.

SMOKED FISH KEBBEH SMØRREBRØD

WITH ORANGE BLOSSOM

serves 6–8
prep   20 minutes
cook   25 minutes

1 small onion, roughly
  chopped
240 g (8½ oz/1⅓ cups)
  very fine burghul
zest of 1 orange
1 teaspoon smoked paprika
pinch of ground allspice
pinch of ground cinnamon
1 teaspoon ground turmeric
400 g (14 oz) mixed salmon
  and smoked haddock
1 anchovy (optional)
1 tablespoon orange
  blossom water
3 tablespoons olive oil, plus
  extra for greasing
flaky sea salt and freshly
  ground black pepper
50 g (1¾ oz/⅓ cup)
  almonds, toasted, to serve

for the charred vegetables:
2 tablespoons olive oil
1 yellow (bell) pepper,
  thinly sliced
1 courgette (zucchini),
  thinly sliced
1 aubergine (eggplant),
  thinly sliced
1 large red onion,
  thinly sliced
2 preserved lemons, flesh
  and seeds discarded, rinds
  thinly sliced

for the coriander tarator:
2 garlic cloves, peeled
  and crushed
2 tablespoons tahini
2 tablespoons coriander
  (cilantro), finely chopped
juice of 1 lemon

The coast running all along the western edge of Lebanon offers up two ingredients: fish and citrus, which in turn makes for a local staple, the fragrant fish kebbeh. A good kebbeh is a subtle dance of flavours – there are no overpowering spices here.

This is excellent for casual alfresco gatherings, and is great make-ahead fare. You can freeze it cooked or uncooked and heat through before serving. It is best eaten warm or at room temperature.

In a small food processor, blitz the onion to a fine paste. Remove and strain, keeping the juices and purée separate.

Add the burghul to a large mixing bowl and use your hands to rub in the reserved onion juices, spices, orange zest and salt and pepper, then pour over 200 ml (7 fl oz/generous ¾ cup) water. Use a fork to fluff and set aside for about 10 minutes.

Make the tarator. Combine the ingredients with 60 ml (2 fl oz/¼ cup) water in a mixing bowl. Season with salt, then taste and adjust the seasoning as needed. Cover and set aside.

Preheat the oven to 200°C/400°F/Gas 6.

Return to the burghul, which should have absorbed all of the water. If not, squeeze out the excess water very well. Taste and adjust the seasoning.

Finely chop the salmon and haddock and place in a mixing bowl with the burghul, puréed onion, and anchovy if using. Return the mixture to the food processor, in batches, pulsing it to produce a fine paste. Once the mixture has become a cohesive paste, be careful not to overwork it. This process should take 2–3 minutes. Return the fish paste to a bowl and add the orange blossom water, mixing well to combine. At this stage, you can pinch off a small piece and quickly fry it in a small frying pan until cooked. Taste. Adjust the seasoning of the fish paste to your preference.

To a small bowl, add some water and ice cubes (this keeps your fingers cool while handling the fish paste and makes spreading a little easier). Grease a 30 x 22 cm (12 x 9 in) shallow baking dish with oil. Spread the fish paste out onto the base of the greased dish, creating a thin, even layer. Dip your fingers into the bowl of iced water to help when spreading the dough, but you just want drops of water on your fingers or else the mixture becomes too wet. Brush generously with 3 tablespoons oil. Place a sheet of baking (parchment) paper on top followed by dried pulses of baking beans and blind bake in the oven for about 15 minutes, until the kebbeh appears cooked through.

While the kebbeh is cooking, in a mixing bowl, toss the vegetables in the oil. Preheat a chargrill pan over high heat. Add the vegetables in batches and cook until nicely charred, about 10–15 minutes. Remove from the heat and set aside.

To serve, layer the vegetables on top of the kebbeh. Drizzle over the tarator and scatter with toasted almonds.

CANDIED BEETROOT MAQLUBA

WITH SMOKED MACKEREL & ORANGE BLOSSOM

serves   6–8
prep   10 minutes
cook   30 minutes

1 x quantity parboiled rice
   (page 216)
2 garlic cloves, peeled and
   finely chopped
zest of 1 orange
1–2 tablespoons orange
   blossom water
flaky sea salt and freshly
   ground black pepper
1 teaspoon ground turmeric
125 g (4 oz) smoked
   mackerel, broken into
   pieces
45 ml (1½ fl oz) rapeseed oil
400 g (14 oz) mixed candied
   beetroot (beet) and regular
   beetroot, peeled and cut
   into 5 mm (¼ in) slices
40 g (1½ oz) butter

Ah, the magnificent maqluba, layers of aromatic spiced rice made with minced meat and vegetables. It's a sight to see and a grace of the *aazeemeh* table. My version of this one-pot meal adds a nice colour injection through the use of candied beetroot and offers up fish as an alternative to the more traditional lamb or chicken. However, you can substitute the mackerel with lamb or chicken, if you prefer. For a vegetarian version or to serve the rice alongside other proteins, omit the mackerel and bulk it up with cauliflower or aubergines (eggplant).

In a bowl, combine the rice with the garlic, orange zest and orange blossom water, and season with salt and pepper. Remove 3–4 tablespoons of the rice and place in a small mixing bowl with the turmeric. To the rest of the rice, add in the mackerel. Cover and set aside.

Add the oil and 2–3 tablespoons water to a heavy-based saucepan with a lid and place over medium-low heat. Arrange the beetroot slices on the base of the pan, starting with the red ones from the outside and the whiter/yellower ones inside, overlapping as you go. Sprinkle over the rice, then use the handle end of a spoon to make three indents, without piercing through the beetroot layer. Wrap the lid of the pan in a clean tea towel and tie it into a tight knot at the handle, then cover the pan (the tea towel will prevent the moisture from dripping into the rice and making it soggy). Reduce the heat to low and cook for 20–30 minutes. Remove from the heat and allow to rest for 5 minutes.

Once rested, remove the lid and carefully flip onto a large serving plate. The maqluba won't turn over in a tidy manner, so don't worry. Just feel free to reposition the beetroot accordingly.

SALMON FEAST:

ROASTED SALMON'S HEAD, SKIN-WRAPPED MILIEU & SEARED TAIL

serves 8–10 as part of a multi-course menu
prep 45–50 minutes
cook 1 hour

for the fish head ghalieh with tamarind and fenugreek:
250 g (9 oz) pre-packaged tamarind pulp
1 salmon head
80 ml (2½ fl oz/ ⅓ cup) rapeseed oil
1 large onion, finely chopped
1 teaspoon ground turmeric
1 small hot red chilli, deseeded and finely chopped
1 tablespoon fenugreek seeds
2 handfuls coriander (cilantro) leaves, finely chopped
1–2 handfuls parsley leaves, finely chopped
1 garlic head, peeled and finely chopped
Tahdeeg rice (page 213 and pages 217–218), to serve

A fish in three parts is a conversation starter – and requires far less effort than it sounds. First, go for a wild fish, if you can. I love salmon for its fatty meat but I treat myself to it only occasionally because of the unsustainability of farming practices.

The head is the best part. It's the sweetest, most succulent, most nutritious meat, especially the rapture-rousing flesh on the cheek and the collar bone. While not exactly made as Al Baghdadi had suggested, the recipe is in fact inspired by one in his 13th-century *Book of Dishes* that called for a fish; 'Whose head is roasted, whose middle is baked and whose tail is fried'. In my version, the Persian curry *ghalieh* (which is also a hit at my supperclubs) supplies adventurous eaters a more enticing dining experience. I've accounted for extra sauce as it can be enjoyed across the different thematic parts of this fish, should you wish.

A 2 kg (4 lb 6 oz) whole salmon should feed 6–8 people, alongside other side dishes. Ask your fishmonger to prepare the salmon into the following parts: head reserved, tail reserved (skin on), and two fillets, skins reserved. See picture overleaf.

Put the tamarind pulp in a large heatproof bowl, pour over 480 ml (16 fl oz) just-boiled water and leave to soak for about 10 minutes. With a fork, mash the tamarind until it dissolves in the water, leaving you with a thick, sauce-like paste. Strain through a fine sieve, discarding the seeds and tough fibres. Set aside.

Preheat the oven to 180°C/350°F/Gas 4. Line a baking sheet with baking (parchment) paper and lightly grease with oil.

for the skin-wrapped
salmon milieu with
vegetables:
2 skins of the salmon
600–800 kg (1 lb 5 oz–
  1 lb 12 oz) whole side of
  salmon, skin removed and
  reserved
2½ tablespoons extra virgin
  olive oil, plus extra to
  grease
3–4 radishes, thinly sliced
3–4 small purple potatoes,
  very thinly sliced
1 carrot, peeled and thinly
  sliced
½ leek, thinly sliced
½ fennel bulb, thinly sliced
  lengthways
5 cherry tomatoes, sliced

for the salmon tail with
date molasses and toasted
sesame seeds:
1 salmon tail, skin-on, pat dry
  using paper towels
45–60 ml (1½–2 fl oz)
  rapeseed oil
1 tablespoon Bezar spice mix
  (page 28)
1–2 tablespoons date
  molasses
2 tablespoons sesame
  seeds, toasted
flaky sea salt and freshly
  ground black pepper

Heat the remaining oil in a large, heavy-based saucepan over medium-low heat. Add the onion and fry for 3 minutes until translucent and lightly brown. Add the turmeric, chilli and fenugreek, and cook for a further 3–4 minutes, until aromatic. Add the coriander, parsley and garlic and cook for 2–3 minutes, until the herbs wilt and darken in colour, stirring often. Add the tamarind paste and reduce the heat to low. Partially cover with the lid and simmer for 30 minutes.

For the skin-wrapped salmon milieu, lay the salmon skins vertically on the prepared baking sheet. Place the salmon on top, so it is horizontal on skin, and season with salt and pepper and half the oil. Arrange the vegetables around the salmon, brush with the remaining oil and season with salt and pepper. Fold the edges of the salmon skins onto the salmon. The skin should partially cover the salmon, like in the picture on the following page.

Next, generously brush the salmon head with the rapeseed oil and place on a separate baking tray. Roast both the salmon and head for 25–30 minutes, or until the vegetables are tender, the salmon cooked through and the skin crisp.

During the final 5 minutes of the roast salmon, prepare the salmon tail with date molasses. Place a non-stick frying pan over medium heat and add 2 tablespoons of rapeseed oil. Season the salmon tail with salt, pepper and the bazaar spices, and brush the skin with more oil. Place the tail, skin-side down, into the pan and sear on each side for about 3 minutes, until the skin has crisped up and the flesh is almost cooked through. Repeat for the other side, searing for another 3 minutes until the flesh has cooked through.

Transfer the salmon tail to a serving plate, drizzle with the date molasses and toasted sesame seeds. Stand the salmon head on a serving plate and spoon the sauce around it. Slice portions of the skin-wrapped salmon into individual portions. Serve everything with Tahdeeg rice (page 213) or a vegetarian Beetroot maqluba (page 224).

SALT-CRUSTED FLAMING BIRD

STUFFED WITH SPICED BANANA, CHESTNUT & SUJUK

serves 4–6
prep   40 minutes
cook   1 hour
        plus 30 minutes

1.5 kg (3 lb 5 oz) chicken or
   duck
152 g (5⅓ oz/about 5) egg
   whites
1.5 kg (3 lb 4 oz) fine sea salt
8 star anise, ground
10 cardamom pods, seeds
   removed and ground
60 ml (2 fl oz/¼ cup) rum
   (optional)

for the stuffing:
2 teaspoons butter
2 shallots, finely chopped
1 garlic head, cloves peeled
   and finely chopped
50 g (1¾ oz) sujuk or streaky
   bacon, chopped
100 g (3½ oz) finely
   chopped apple
60 g (2 oz) finely chopped
   banana
60 g (2 oz) fresh
   breadcrumbs
½ teaspoon
   ground cardamom
½ teaspoon ground aniseed
¼ teaspoon
   ground cinnamon
pinch of ground nutmeg
pinch of ground cloves
¼ teaspoon ground ginger
100 ml (3⅓ fl oz) rum
50 g (1¾ oz) cooked
   vacuum-packed
   chestnuts, chopped
flaky sea salt and freshly
   ground black pepper

Do not let the sound of this recipe put you off. It's really simple to make. The Turkish *tuzda tavuk* from Hatay, which the recipe is based on, dates back to the Ottoman period, perhaps inspired through Chinese migration and their method of baking fowl in a salt crust. I quite like the unconventional inclusion of banana in the stuffing. Give it a try, it's quite subtle and keeps the chicken moist.

I prefer to use fine sea salt for the salt crust. It creates a more cohesive mixture, making moulding easier. Feel free to decorate the salt crust with spices or either of the seasoned salts in chapter 3 (page 67).

Make the stuffing. Melt the butter in a saucepan, add the shallots and sauté over medium-low heat for 3–4 minutes, until soft and translucent. Stir in the garlic and cook for a further minute, until aromatic. Add the sujuk and brown for 1–2 minutes, stirring often. Toss in the apple, banana, breadcrumbs and spices, and mix well to combine. Lightly season with salt, then pour over the rum. Reduce the heat to medium and cook, stirring often, until the mixture is soft and spongy, about 6–8 minutes. Add the chestnuts, stir, taste and adjust the seasoning. Remove from the heat and allow to cool.

Preheat the oven to 200°C/400°F/Gas 6 .

Place the chicken on a large plate and stuff the cavity with most or all of the stuffing. Whisk the egg whites in a large mixing bowl, then add the salt and ground spices, then mix well to combine. The mixture should feel like wet sand. Place a couple of handfuls of the salt on the centre of a baking tray. Place the stuffed chicken on top, then use your hands to mould the remaining salt and spices mixture all over the chicken, making sure it is completely and evenly covered, with no protruding parts of chicken. Bake in the oven for 1½ hours, or until the chicken is cooked through. You can check the chicken is done by carefully inserting a meat thermometer through the crust. It should register at 75°C/165°F.

Once the chicken is cooked, remove from the oven. If using rum, pour it all over the chicken, then use a blow torch to flame it until you have a burnished, golden crust. Leave the chicken to sit for a few minutes, then crack the salt open using a knife or the back of a wooden spoon. Discard the salt crust and brush away any excess salt. Leave to rest for a further 5 minutes, then serve immediately.

Also try: You can also use the stuffing in a duck or turkey. Double the recipe if you're opting for a medium-sized duck or turkey.

DEWY QUAIL & MUTTON MANDI

WITH SMOKED BASMATI RICE

serves   8–10
prep   20 minutes
cook   2–3 hours

2–3 tablespoons Aged butter
(page 29) or regular butter

4–6 large mutton or lamb
shanks, brought to room
temperature

4–6 quails, spatchcocked
(ask your butcher to do
this)

2 onions, finely chopped

1 garlic head, peeled and
finely sliced

600 g (1 lb 5 oz) basmati rice,
rinsed and drained

2 tablespoons Hawayej spice
mix (page 28)

1–2 bay leaves

1.2 litres (51 fl oz/6 cups)
light stock or water

2 tablespoons raisins

3–4 tablespoons toasted
cashews

3–4 tablespoons toasted
almonds

3–4 tablespoons toasted
pine nuts

handful parsley, finely
chopped

Maldon smoked sea salt

Smoked tomato hot sauce
(page 76) or hot sauce,
to serve (optional)

The traditional dish of the Hadhramaut region in Yemen, mandi is
one of the many spiced rice and meat dishes ubiquitous to the region.
Mandi is a rather specialised concoction, however, as the method
calls for slow-cooking meat that is suspended over an open pot of rice
in a tandoor oven heated by amber. The smoking process lends the
dish its signature taste and luxuriously moist texture, which inspired
its name. *Mandi* is from the Arabic root word *nada*, meaning 'dew'.
It is not necessary to dig a tandoor oven in your backyard to get the
authentic taste. A little home-style slow-cooking and adaptation will
lend delicious results. You can also buy pre-smoked rice online. For
this recipe, you will need a fairly large ovenproof pan and a circular
wire rack that fits nicely on top. Alternatively, once the aromatics have
cooked and the rice and stock has been added, transfer to a baking tray
and sit a wire rack on top of this. The long and slow cooking of mutton
shanks here is, trust me, a worthwile investment. The gamey flavour of
this finished dish is worth the wait.

Preheat the oven to 150°C/300°F/Gas 1. Generously season the mutton
and quails with smoked sea salt.

Place a large, wide ovenproof pan over medium heat, melt 1 tablespoon
of the butter and brown the shanks in batches, turning them once or twice
to ensure even browning. Repeat the same process with the quails, adding
more butter as needed. Remove and set aside.

Melt a knob of butter in the pan used to brown the meat. Add the onions,
cover with the lid and sweat over low heat for 10–15 minutes, stirring often,
until soft and translucent. Add the garlic and cook for a further minute,
then add the rice, hawayej mix and bay leaves and toss to coat. Allow
everything to lightly brown for a minute or so. Pour in the stock, season
with smoked salt to taste and stir well to combine. Line the shanks up
across the rack, then seal the whole dish very well with foil. Make sure
there are no gaps as the rice needs to steam. Transfer to the oven and
slow-cook for 2–3 hours, until the meat is tender, falling off the bone and
the rice has absorbed the water.

for smoking the rice
(optional):
1 coal broquette
a pinch of woodchips

If smoking the rice, remove the tray from the oven, carefully remove the rack with the mutton, set aside. Place a small ramekin in the middle of the rice with a red hot coal inside and a tiny pinch of smoking chips. Return the rack with the mutton on it and seal the dish very well. Set aside for at least 10 minutes to infuse the rice with the smoke.

Meanwhile, increase the oven temperature to 180°C/350°F/Gas 4. Arrange the quail on a baking tray and roast until cooked through and the juices run clear, about 10–15 minutes.

Carefully remove the shanks from the rack and place on a chopping board. Remove the rack and toss the raisins into the rice. Transfer to a large serving platter and then lay the meat on top, alternating between the shanks and the quail. Sprinkle over the toasted nuts and parsley. Serve with smoked tomato hot sauce, if you like.

6

NEVER-ENDING FEAST

SOFRA DAIMEH

Our concept of dessert is quite different from the West's. Sweets 'occupy' an important place in our lives; standing as a symbol of hospitality to greet guests alongside coffee, tea or other sharabs (page 244). Don't expect them every day and to end every meal! Intricate nut-layered and syrup-doused cakes and pastries are often reserved for big celebrations, religious holidays and rites of passage (see meghli on page 247, for example). In the West you may bring wine as a gift to your host, but in the Middle East you may bring sweets (the type dictated by the occasion). Additionally, your host may have made a purchase of his or her own.

Delicate layered pastries, such as baklava, and sweets are not historically the speciality of home-cooks but relegated to the professionals and palace chefs, which kept the recipes mysteriously elusive. However, many home-makers make a few sweet, homemade delights using humble ingredients, like shortbread cookies such as *ma'amoul* and *ghraybeh* (see Virgin's Breasts, page 242), fruit compotes and sorbets and semolina-based cakes (see Helbeh, page 254).

It's no revelation that many Middle Eastern sweets are VERY sickly-sweet, as they tend to be drenched in honey or syrup, a likely consequence of the prohibition (see Al kohl, page 52, and Sugar and spice, page 244). In addition to sugar, sweeteners such as honey and molasses made from carob, dates and grapes continue to be popular and are often preferred after a meal, swirled into tahini, an 'after-eight' praised for its health benefits (see fawakeh mushakala, page 241).

As a lazy sweet maker with a rather mellowed-out sweet tooth – here forth are my simple, quick and sweet-ish offerings.

EAT TOGETHER AND
DO NO SEPARATE,
FOR THE BLESSING (BARAKAH)
IS IN THE COMPANY.

PROPHET MUHAMMAD

FRUIT PLATTER & FRUIT SALAD

Fruit is an important part of a feast's conclusion. For the more casual option, seasonal fruit is served on platters with a knife, alongside clotted cream, honey, tahini, carob and molasses as well as Turkish delight and digestive biscuits. People can help themselves. For a quick dipping sauce, add carob molasses to a bowl and gently swirl in tahini and honey, for some added sweetness.

WHAT YOU'LL OFTEN SEE, DEPENDING ON THE SEASON:

Strawberries

Melon

Avocado

Loquats

Apple Custard

Persimmon

Cherries

Satsumas

Pomegranate

Banana

Figs

Plums

Redcurrants

THE VIRGIN'S BREASTS

WITH LAVENDER

makes 24 cookies
prep 7 minutes
cook 12 minutes

175 g (6 oz/1 cup) unsalted
 butter
225 g (8 oz/1½ cups) plain
 (all-purpose) flour
60 g (2 oz/½ cup) icing
 (confectioner's) sugar
¼ teaspoon lavender,
 ground
⅛ teaspoon frankincense
 essence (optional)
24 shelled unsalted
 pistachios
spray-free rose petals,
 for decoration (optional)

Arab poets have a knack for relating their food to women and their bodily parts, for example the famous 'ladies arms' *(znood el sit)* dessert, or these biscuits. Virgin's breasts comes to us all the way from 14th century Baghdad, though I've added the frankincense and lavender. They are the precursor to the ubiquitous ghraybeh cookies, *ghraybeh* meaning 'to swoon', as you do. Once cooked, the virgin's breasts will flatten a good deal and crumble quite easily at the touch, so perhaps that's how they got their name. In any case, they are as suited to a formal dessert table as to a casual chinwag and are excellent served with Arabic coffee (page 50) or tea (page 47).

Preheat the oven to 200°C/400°F/Gas 6 and line a baking sheet with baking (parchment) paper.

Melt the butter in a small saucepan over medium heat, then add the flour and cook, whisking, for 1 minute. Remove from the heat, add the icing sugar, lavender, frankincense, if using, and whisk. The resulting mixture should be a buttery, soft and slightly wet dough.

Use a tablespoon to portion out 24 even-sized balls, rolling them in the palm of your hands (feel free to lightly flour your hands if the dough gets too sticky). Arrange on the prepared baking sheet, making sure there is a little space between each as they will expand during cooking. Gently lay a pistachio in the centre of each ball – use the slightest pressure rather than pressing down. Bake in the oven for 10–12 minutes, until the edges are slightly golden. Leave to cool, then gently transfer to a serving tray. Serve with rose petals sprinkled over, if you like.

SUGAR AND SPICE
AND EVERYTHING NICE

There was a time when sugar was seductive and nice. Considered a spice, it was valued for its preserving and medicinal properties.

Circa 500 BC, the Emperor Darius of Persia invaded India to find a sweet surprise; 'the reed which gives honey without bees' which was still being extracted via water. A millennia later, the Arabs would invade Persia only to discover the same delight. They would become masters of growing, refining and cooking with sugar, literally sugar-coating food and botanicals beyond medicine or spice, into rare delicacies for wealthy and noble pleasure-seekers.

The Arabs would pioneer syrup ('atr or قطر also known as *sharabat* (شرابات) combining sugar with water to preserve fruit (see Reisling poached pear syrup and rhubarb and rose syrup, page 252), flower extracts and herbs. They used the syrup for many things, including lemon candy – the lemon helping break down the sucrose into fructose and glucose – but preserves, jams and sweetened pastry and dough too. They also used it for sharabs – flavoured syrups, diluted with water and poured over ice or snow, effectively the precursors of modern-day soft drinks (page 54). Sharabs proliferated, perhaps as a result of the Islamic prohibition of alcohol.

Via both the Moors, who conquered North Africa and Spain, and the crusaders returning from the Holy Land, sugar and its sweet everythings would spill over to Europe. Sharab would slowly transform into sorbet (and sherbet) and sugar would ultimately seduce all.

श्कर

ŚARKARĀ

(SANSKRIT FOR PEBBLES)

سكر

SUKKAR

(ARABIC FOR SUGAR)

STICKY FREEZER CAKE

WITH TAHINI & CAROB MOLASSES

serves 8–10
prep 10 minutes,
plus freezing time

300 g (10½ oz) digestive
biscuits
125 g (4 oz/scant 1 cup)
pistachios
700 g (1 lb 9 oz) carob
molasses or grape
molasses
435 g (15½ oz) tahini
3–4 tablespoons runny
honey, optional
3 tablespoons sesame
seeds, toasted
4 tablespoons desiccated
(shredded) coconut

This is a riff on my Aunt Janane's biscuit or fridge cake, which she coined 'gateau Zaza'. Hers is made with chocolate but here I've opted for more heritage ingredients, perhaps even the Middle Eastern equivalent to Nutella or peanut butter and jelly – tahini and molasses. These two ingredients are often served with a fruit platter and simply drizzled over for a low-key dessert. *Debs el kharub* – carob molasses – is considered incredibly healthy. Kick it up a notch in this chilled sticky cake. It's as simple as dessert can get.

To a mixing bowl, add the biscuits and lightly crush them, then stir in pistachios. In a separate bowl, add the carob molasses and ever so gently swirl in the tahini, and honey (if using). Combine the two mixtures, tossing well. It's fine if the biscuits get crushed a little more along the way.

Line a 30 x 18 cm (12 x 7 in) baking tray with baking (parchment) paper, and use a spatula to press the mix down into the tin to form an even, flat surface. Sprinkle over the sesame seeds and desiccated coconut, and then use a sharp knife slice into even squares. Cover with cling film (plastic wrap) and transfer to the freezer for about 1 hour or until set. This cake will keep in the freezer for a couple of months or in the fridge for a week. You can store it either way, depending on whether you prefer the texture softer or harder.

WELCOME-BABY PUDDING

WITH CARAWAY, COCONUT & A CASHEW SURPRISE

serves 8–10
prep 10 minutes
cook 20–30 minutes

200 g (7 oz/scant 1¼ cups)
 rice flour
1 tablespoon ground caraway
1 tablespoon ground
 cinnamon
1 tablespoon ground aniseed
175 g (6 oz/scant 1 cup) soft
 light brown sugar
400 ml (13½ fl oz/1⅔ cups)
 coconut cream
2 tablespoons orange
 blossom water
1 cashew
50 g (1¾ oz) desiccated
 (shredded) coconut
30 g (1 oz/¼ cup) walnuts,
 soaked for 10 minutes and
 skins removed
20–30 g (¾–1 oz) almonds,
 soaked for 10 minutes and
 skins removed
30 g (1 oz/¼ cup) pistachios,
 soaked for 10 minutes and
 skins removed
40 g (1½ oz/¼ cup) raisins,
 soaked for 10 mnutes and
 strained
20 g (¾ oz) pine nuts

Meghli means 'boiled' in Arabic. The name is perhaps fitting as in the original recipe the pudding takes up to an hour to simmer and cook. My version is quicker to prepare. Traditionally, it is made to celebrate the birth of a child and, as such, it's also a regular at the Christmas table to hail the birth of Jesus. Aside from celebrating births, the pudding is thought to benefit the mother, as caraway can improve lactation and reduce bloating. It is very subtle in sweetness. And the caraway is just there as a touch of flavour as it can be overpowering if too much is added.

Place a heavy-based saucepan over medium heat, add the flour, caraway, cinnamon, aniseed, sugar, coconut cream and 800 ml (27 fl oz/3⅓ cups) water, and whisk to combine. Stir, uncovered, as it bubbles, squeaks and thickens. Reduce the heat to a simmer and cook for 20 minutes, stirring very often, and whisking occasionally to make sure any lumps are broken down. The mixture should thicken to a mashed potato consistency. Remove from the heat and stir in the orange blossom water. Cover and set aside for 5–10 minutes to cool.

Spoon the mixture into glass ramekins. Line up eight 175 ml (6 fl oz) glass serving bowls or 10 smaller serving bowls (about 125 ml/4 fl oz/½ cup). Place a cashew surprise in any one of the serving bowls, then divide the mixture evenly across all the ramekins. Sprinkle over the desiccated coconut. Next, place one whole walnut into the centre of each. Add four almonds opposite each other, then in the squares between them, add a few pistachios and raisins. Finally, sprinkle over the pine nuts. If you prefer, you can serve the pudding warm. I much prefer it cold. In the latter case, cover with cling film (plastic wrap), transfer to the fridge until chilled. This dessert can be kept in the fridge for up to a week.

RHUBARB & ROSE MASCARPONE CREAM OSMALIEH

serves 8–10
prep 30 minutes
cook 30 minutes

300 g (10½ oz/2 cups) kataifi
(shredded filo pastry)
150 g (5 oz/⅔ cup) unsalted
butter, melted

for the rhubarb syrup (you
can make this a day ahead):
400 g rhubarb (14 oz),
slivered 0.5 cm, plus 1 stick,
shaved and reserved to
decorate (optional)
juice of 1 lemon
100 g (3½ oz/½ cup) caster
(superfine) sugar
2 tablespoons rosewater

for the mascarpone cream
(best made on the day,
though can be made ahead):
500 g (1 lb, 2 oz/2 cups)
mascarpone
250 ml (8 fl oz/1 cup)
whipping cream
75 g (2½ oz/½ cup) icing
(confectioner's) sugar
1 teaspoon ground
cardamom
2 tablespoons rose water

for the garnish:
rhubarb peel, macerated in a
tablespoon of sugar
50 g (2 oz/⅓ cup) pistachios,
crushed

Knafeh, from the Arabic root *kanaf* comes to mean 'to enclose something', the dish dates back to 9th century Baghdad caliphate. Indeed, a variety of fillings are enclosed in a variety of crusts and moulded into a variety of shapes and sizes. Enjoyed sizzling hot or cold depending on the filling, the crust can be made with semolina (fine knafeh), shredded (coarse knafeh) or a combination thereof (wavering knafeh) or rolled into fingers or cones. My recipe here can also be adapted into individual-serve cakes if the occasion calls for it. All elements can be prepared a day ahead and assembled at serving.

This specific version is known as *Osmalieh* or 'of the Ottomans' in the Levant, which calls for clotted cream and the filo strings, which may or may not be shredded fine. It's an excellent cake for gatherings, that actually doesn't need much time to bring together. The flavourings can be tweaked to use up the best of what's in season. See Labneh mousse (page 252) for more ideas.

Start with a small amount of rosewater and then gradually increase – it should be fragrant enough to contrast the mousse without overpowering it.

Preheat the oven to 180°C/350°F/Gas 4.

Divide the kataifi into evenly between two bowls. You may also divide the melted butter into two equal portions if you prefer. Working with each portion at a time, butter your fingers and pull apart the kataifi threads very gently to keep their lengths, ensuring they are buttered and seperated. You don't have to be methodical, but the idea is to get the kataifi threads moist.

Take two 20 cm (8 in) cake tins and into each 'snake' in half of the buttered kataifi threads, to create an even base, packing them down to compact them. Bake for 30 minutes, until golden brown and crisp. Remove and set aside to cool.

Meanwhile, into a saucepan, add the slivered rhubarb, lemon juice and caster sugar. Stir and cook over medium heat until the rhubarb releases its juices and is cooked but still retains its shape. Gently stir the mixture, often. This should take about 20 minutes. Remove from the heat, strain the rhubarb and reserve the juice or syrup. Set the rhubarb aside in the fridge to cool. Return the rhubarb juice or syrup to the pan, over low heat, and cook down a further 10 minutes. Pour over the rosewater. Set aside.

To a small mixing bowl, add the whipping cream, icing sugar, cardamom and whip to a soft peak. Remove the reserved rhubarb from the fridge, keeping one third of it aside for final decorations. Add the mascarpone to a mixing bowl, add in two thirds of the cooked rhubarb, the rosewater and fold in the whipped cream.

Transfer a kataifi base to a serving or cake plate. Spoon over the mascarpone cream, spreading it carefully and then add the top layer of the kataifi. Press it down very, very gently, just to sandwich it. Use the back of the spoon to go around the cream and soften the edges. Press into the cream the reserved rhubarb to create a pretty visual. Sprinkle over the crushed pistachios and arrange the shaved rhubarb in the middle. Serve with the syrup in a pouring 'cup' on the side, preferably slightly warm.

BLACK MAGIC BROWNIES

WITH NIGELLA SEEDS & CLEMENTINE

serves   6–8
prep   10 minutes
cook   20 minutes

300 g (10½ oz/2 cups) plain
  (all-purpose) flour, lightly
  toasted
85 ml (2¾ fl oz/½ cup) olive
  oil
1 teaspoon mustard seeds,
  crushed
150 g (5 fl oz/scant ½ cup)
  honey
7 clementines, yielding
  250 ml (8½ fl oz/1 cup)
  juice, or orange juice
zest of 1–2 clementines, or
  1 orange
35 g (1¼ oz/scant ¼ cup)
  blanched almonds

for the nigella seed paste:
165 g (6 oz) nigella seeds
100 ml (3½ fl oz) neutral
  oil such as rapeseed or
  sunflower oil

'There is healing in black seed for all diseases except death' as Prophet Muhammad said about nigella seeds. This miracle seed has now gained traction as a trendy cure among modern health gurus. Known as *habt el barakah,* or 'seed of blessing', it remains in popular use in the Middle East, sprinkled onto breads and into pastry fillings. It is also used to make a slightly more obscure paste known as *qizha* in South Lebanon and Palestine. For these black magic brownies I have repurposed the paste. The nigella seeds impart a distinct flavour and colour and I have found the addition of clementine lends a welcome tangy-sweet dimension. It's an intriguingly delightful treat.

Make the nigella seed paste by blitzing the ingredients in a food processor until smooth. Set aside.

Preheat the oven to 180°C/350°F/Gas 4. Line a 28 x 20 cm (11 x 8 in) baking tray with baking (parchment) paper.

Add the flour to a mixing bowl and drizzle in the olive oil. Mix together well with a fork, then add the mustard seeds, honey, clementine juice and zest and nigella paste, and mix until well combined.

Pour the mixture into the prepared tray. Use a knife to slice the mixture into diamond-shaped pieces, or rectangular brownie-like pieces, then press an almond into the centre of each shape. Bake in the oven for 15–20 minutes, or until firm to the touch, or a wooden skewer or toothpick comes out clean once inserted.

CHOCOLATE CRUMB LABNEH MOUSSE

WITH PEARS POACHED IN A MASTIC & RIESLING SYRUP

serves   6-8
prep   10 minutes
cook   30 minutes

for the mousse:
150 g (5½ oz/1¼ cups) icing
   (confectioner's) sugar
300 ml (10½ fl oz/1¼ cups)
   double (heavy) cream
500 g (1 lb 2 oz/2 cups) full-
   fat Greek (FAGE®) yoghurt
   (or soft labneh, page 25)
100 g (3½ oz) 80% dark
   chocolate, crushed

for poaching the pears:
4-6 small pears, peeled with
   stalks left intact
2 tablespoons lemon juice
500 ml riesling
½ tsp ground mastic (about
   2 medium tears)
250 g (9 oz/generous cup)
   caster (superfine) sugar
1 tablespoon orange
   blossom water

This is my go-to no-fuss dessert. The beauty is that it's simple, refreshing, and ever-so versatile. I just incorporate spices, and fruit based on season. Try it also using sour cherries and *mahlab* (an aromatic spice made from cherry stones), apple and rose, or dried figs and star anise. You can also use quince or apple in place of the pears.

Peel and quarter the pears and then immediately brush them with lemon juice to stop them oxidising. In a heavy-based saucepan over medium heat, combine the riesling, ground mastic, caster sugar and 125 ml (4 oz/ ½ cup) of water, bring to a simmer then add the pears. Poach for about 20 minutes over gentle heat, until tender but still holding their shape. Using a slotted spoon, remove the pears and set aside. Bring the mixture to a boil and then reduce again and simmer the sugar syrup for about 10 minutes, or until thickened slightly. Mix in orange blossom water. To test if it's done, put a teaspoon of the mixture on a plate and leave to cool for a minute. It should be jam-like in consistency. Set aside to cool slightly.

Meanwhile, in a mixing bowl, whisk the ground mastic, icing sugar and cream to soft peaks. Fold into the yoghurt, with the crushed chocolate and set aside.

Divide the labneh mousse among 6-8 serving bowls. Top with the poached pears and drizzle over with the reisling syrup. You can prepare this two days in advance and store, covered, in the fridge.

ROLLED DAMASK BUCHE

WITH PERSIMMON & PISTACHIO ICE CREAM

serves 12
prep 25 minutes,
plus freezing

450 g (1 lb) persimmon
flesh (2 well-ripened
persimmons)
1 litre (34 fl oz/4 cups) full-fat
milk
750 ml (25½ fl oz/3 cups)
double (heavy) cream
300 g (10½ oz/1⅓ cups)
caster (superfine) sugar
1½ tablespoons ground
salep or cornflour
(cornstarch)
1–2 mastic tears
1 tablespoon finely chopped
ginger
200 g (7 oz/1⅓ cups)
pistachios, finely chopped

When Arabic ice cream – *bouza* – is made using *salep*, a flour from a wild orchid, and then pounded, it is called *boozet el da' or,* loosely, 'pounded ice cream'. This is a hangover from pre-electric days when the mixture was prepared in a metal container placed in a wooden barrel filled with ice and salt and pounded with a long-handled mallet. Here's a home-friendly version. If the rolled buche is a bit much, you can churn the two mixtures in an ice cream machine, and simply scoop and serve. The salep and mastic give it a stretchy, chewy texture.

Using a spatula, press the persimmon flesh through a fine sieve into a bowl. Discard the tough bits that remain in the sieve.

Place a large, heavy-based pan over medium heat. Pour in the milk, cream, sugar, salep and mastic tears and whisk constantly and vigorously for 10–15 minutes, letting it very gently simmer, until thickened and coats the back of a spoon. Transfer 375 ml (12½ fl oz/2½ cups) of the mixture to a large bowl and whisk in the puréed persimmon and ginger.

Line two rectangular baking trays (one 25 x 30 cm/10 x 12 in and one 30 x 36 cm/12 x 14 in) with cling film (plastic wrap). Pour the persimmon mixture into the smaller tray, leveling the mixture out with a spatula. Cover with more plastic wrap, making sure it is very well sealed and lie flat in the freezer. Repeat with the milk mixture, using the larger tray. Leave in the freezer for about 6 hours, until completely frozen.

Remove the ice cream from the freezer, transfer to a large bowl and pound it using a pestle. Spread the chopped pistachios onto cling film in the tray, then, working carefully but quickly, lay the ice cream on top, pressing down gently to cover the nuts. Cover it very well and transfer to the freezer for about 4 hours or until solid. Remove the persimmon ice cream and repeat the pounding technique. Spread it across the tray lined with cling film, cover it well and return to the freezer for another 4 hours or until solid. Peel away the cling film from the milk ice cream and remove the persimmon ice cream from its tray using the cling film, invert it over the milk ice cream, then peel away the remaining cling film. Working from one of the shorter edges, roll the two ice creams into a log. Cover tightly with cling film and store in the freezer. Serve this as a log to be sliced at the table or pre-sliced.

FENUGREEK, KEFIR & HONEY SEMOLINA CARROT CAKE

serves 8–10
prep   10 minutes
cook   30–40 minutes

for the cake:
200 g (7 oz/1 cup) mixed
  heritage carrots
300 g (10 oz/1¼ cups) fine
  semolina flour
2 teaspoons bicarbonate of
  soda (baking soda)
1 teaspoon fine sea salt
pinch of cinnamon
pinch of nutmeg
1 teaspoon ground fenugreek
100 ml (3¼ fl oz/½ cup)
  olive oil
225 g (8 oz/1 cup) honey
160 ml (5 fl oz/¾ cup) kefir
zest of 1 lemon

for the frosting:
225 g (8 oz/1 cup) full-fat
  Greek (FAGE®) yoghurt
  (or soft labneh, page 25)
1–2 tablespoons honey

for the topping:
100 g (3½ oz/½ cup) mixed
  heritage carrots
3–4 tablespoons flaked
  almonds, toasted

This is my favourite take on the traditional semolina-based cakes of the region; *merging helbeh* aka fenugreek cake with the carrot cake and adding kefir to incorporate moisture and fluffiness (though you can use FAGE® yoghurt or labneh, page 28). I've also dropped the overly sweet syrup ubiquitous to these cakes, making it less sickly than the traditional version. You can use a mix of heritage carrots to get a contrast of colour, especially for the honeyed carrot thins on top. This is a wonderful cake to make when you're in a rush but want something delicious or while a stew slow cooks. The perfect everyday treat, triple the recipe to make a beautiful three-tiered cake for special occasions.

Preheat the oven to 180°C/350°F/Gas 4. Grease a 22 cm (8½ in) square baking tin with a little butter and line the base with baking (parchment) paper.

Using a vegetable peeler, shave each heritage carrot lengthways, into thin translucent ribbons. You'll need a generous handful. Transfer to a small mixing bowl and cover with hot water. Shred the remaining carrots, half using the thicker holes and the other in the smaller holes.

In another mixing bowl, combine the semolina flour, bicarbonate of soda, salt, cinnamon, nutmeg and fenugreek. Drizzle over the olive oil and using a fork, make sure the semolina soaks up all the oil and fluff it up. In a separate mixing bowl, combine the kefir, honey and shredded carrots and mix well to combine then stir into the semolina mixture. Pour the mixture into the prepared baking tin and shake gently to even out the surface. Bake for 30–40 minutes, or until a skewer inserted into the middle comes out clean.

Meanwhile, in a medium mixing bowl, whip the yoghurt or labneh with 1 tablespoon of the honey. Set aside in the fridge. Strain the carrot thins, pat dry and then toss in the remaining of honey. Set aside.

Remove the cake from the oven, leave to cool for 20–30 minutes, gently peeling off the baking paper (parchment) within 10 minutes. Turn the cake out onto a plate and spread the frosting across, evenly covering the edges. Sprinkle over the toasted almonds then top with the honeyed carrot ribbons in the centre.

THE MIDDLE EASTERN SOBHIEH

MORNING

I

ROUND-FOR-COFFEE SOBHIEH

Arabic tea or coffee
page 47 or 50

Date, mint and pistachio labneh crumble
page 98

Aysh pita pyramids
page 31

Fruit platter
page 239

The virgin's breasts
page 241

In the West, you have ladies who lunch, in the Middle East, you have ladies who *Sobhieh*. Sobhieh, or the morning break, is the all-important time when women of the house traditionally gather after finishing their morning chores, including having placed the stew on the stove-top to cook in time for lunch. Ladies in the community would gather at a designated home for as little as 20 minutes, or up to an hour, over coffee, indulge in small savoury and sweet nibbles, exchange advice and gossip. Sobhieh's can be informal or formal. Here are some ideas.

2

DESPERATE HOUSEWIVES SOBHIEH

3

FRIENDS-NEVER-LEFT SOBHIEH (AKA THE HANGOVER BRUNCH)

EVERYDAY HUSTLE

LUNCH OR DINNER

I

LIGHT AND QUICK TO THROW-TOGETHER

In the Middle East, *hawader* or *pret-a-manger* foods are not only reserved for the *aazeemeh* but rather work as the fallback ready-meal, freezer dinner and salads in a jar! Here are recipes that can come together quickly or are easy to cook in batches to have-on-hand for a 'rainy' day. If you have a slow-cooker, then get it going in the morning and a warming and hearty dinner will welcome you home! The idea is to choose your main from the options listed and then bulk up the meal with the any of the suggestions in the 'Make it an every-day feast' section.

2

USING YOUR PANTRY, FREEZER OR *PRET-A-MANGER*

3

QUICK STEWS & SLOW-COOKER FRIENDLY DISHES

make it an every-day feast

Decorate the table with a selection of pickles (page 87, 88 and 92), olives, cheese and strained yoghurts (page 25), seasonal herbs or greens (page 140) and some warmed Mini Arabic bread puffs (page 30) or bread of choice.

SOMETHING IN-BETWEEN

AFTERNOON TEA OR
EL AASROUNIEH

OASIS FOUND

DECORATE THE TABLE

SOMETHING SWEET

Traditionally, *aasrounieh* or 'of dusk', is the evening's little nibble. The main feature is a savoury bread, known as *ka'ak el asrounieh* which is served, alongside za'atar, labneh, honey, and, more recently, Nutella. If you have some to hand, you can stuff the pockets with any of those. Alternatively, you can opt for the Mini Arabic bread puffs (page 30) sprinkled with toasted sesame seeds before baking and then stuffing it.

MEZZE MANIA

It's imperative to emphasise that *mazzat* (plural for mezze dishes) – while they bare some resemblance to tapas, appetisers, or antipasti – are, in fact, entirely different in concept and philosophy. Unlike tapas; mezze is not bar food or intermediary nibbles to hold you out until dinner or the main meal. Nor are they appetisers, antipasti or hors d'oeuvre – a sort of small starter or meal course, designed to whet the appetite. But rather, a mezze table is an entire meal made up of small dishes served in a procession (of the bounty that you crave or can afford) beginning with cold or room temperature dishes, such as raw and cooked salads, dips, pastries, which are typical fare in the home cooking of the region. Next comes the hot dishes namely grills – whether seafood, chicken or meat. These grills only start when the diner summons the waiter to start 'the grills or hot food', which could happen as late as an hour or two into the meal. To finish off, something to sweeten the tooth is served alongside tea or coffee. A mezze meal is meant to spread out over an afternoon or an evening – nothing is to be rushed – it's a social affair, reserved for weekends and hosted at dedicated dining establishments. . In fact, when we sit down on the mezze table, one might hear someone say '3 am *mazmeez*' or, 'I'm nibbling.' For as difficult as it is to resist devouring the food, nibble you must, if you are to truly enjoy a mezze spread. In this way, mezze is more comparable to the Scandanavian smorgasbord. A wonderful dining experience, mezze is only one element of the Middle Eastern dinner table, mainly reserved for restaurants because of the sheer level of undertaking required to deliver such an elaborate experience.

OASIS FOUND

Foggy meadow

DECORATE THE TABLE

Artichoke stuffed with green kishk mutabal

Assortment of fatayer

UNFASTEN THE APPETITE

NEVER-ENDING FEAST

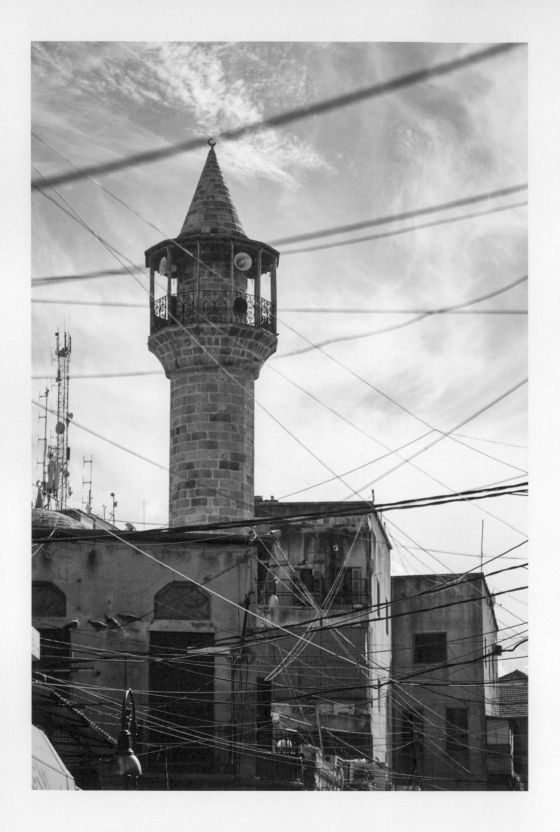

THANK YOU

Writing cookbooks is both a personal experience that is very much inspired by one's own curiosity and observations but also fuelled by research, collection both of personal memory, as well as literary borrowing and appropriation from past and present with doses of creativity, imagination & invention towards a new vision and expectation. It also takes a village to bring a book together and I am indeed indebted to a village of people.

I would like to thank greatly my family; dad, mom, Adla, Joslin, Eli, Chris, Jim, Joyce, Patrick, Melanie, Amouleh, Janane, Joumana and Najwa for their help, support and input.

My taste Lebanon team; Iffat Saadeh and Hisham Assad for having my back and treating the tours as their own which has allowed me to focus on the task at hand.

My manager Annecka Kelleher for her belief and support in this book and finding the right publisher. I am grateful to see this book published with Hardie Grant under the guidance of Kate Pollard. I can't thank you enough for allowing the book to have its personality and voice. My editors Kate Wanwimolruk, Molly Ahuja, as well as Emma and the rest of the Hardie Grant team. Evi O for her patience and care and for bringing together such a beautiful book. Emily Jonsen food stylist extraordinaire and Nassima Rothacker for not settling until you got the shot.

Near and far friends who have patiently been sounding boards, answered my ceaseless questions, advised and influenced or facilitated the book in one way or another and generally been a heavy dose of support when all seemed pointless; Danelle Scott, Judy Cogan, Greg Malouf, Kelley Ralph, Lucy-Ann Gostanian, Dhabia & Wid Al Bayaty, Anto Yerganian, Cindy Nehme, Shaima Saleh, Jason Lee, Joseph Boufarah, Susie Masiello, Ken Miles, Zara Seenaa, Gizem Haskokar and Wines of Lebanon, the Touma family Nathalie and Joe-Assaad of the wonderful St Thomas. I am also indebted to the authors whose own writing has inspired and informed my writing, namely Nawal Nasrallah, Rachel Laudan, Charles Perry, Sami Zubaida to name a few.

Last but not least, thank you for buying this book and your support in helping spread a positive word and image about Middle Eastern food and heritage.

BIBLIOGRAPHY

- *A Baghdad Cookery Book* by Charles Perry
- *A Taste of Thyme. Culinary Cultures of the Middle East* by Sami Zubaida
- *Annals of the Caliph's Kitchens* by Nawal Nasrallah
- AramcoWorld.com
- *Cuisine & Empire: Cooking in World History* by Rachel Lauden
- *Delights from the Garden of Eden: A Cookbook and History of the Iraqi Cuisine* by Nawal Nasrallah
- *Feast: Why Humans Share Food* by Martin Jones
- *Food, Feasts, and Faith: An Encyclopaedia of Food Culture in World Religions* by Paul Fieldhouse
- *Linguistic Convergence & Areal Diffusion: Case Studies from Iranian, Semitic and Turkic*
- *Medieval Arab Cookery* by Maxime Rodinson, AJ Arberry & Charles Perry
- *Medieval Cuisine of the Islamic world: A Concise History with 174 Recipes* by Lilia Zaouali
- *Middle Mongolian Loan Words in Volga Kipchak Languages* by Eva Csaki
- *The Jewelled Kitchen* by Bethany Kehdy
- *The Oldest Cuisine in the World: Cooking in Mesopotamia* by Jean Bottero
- *The Oxford Companion to Food The Oxford Companion to Food* by Alan Davidson & Tom Jaine
- *The Silk Roads: A New History of the World* by Peter Frankopan
- *Oxford Symposium On Food & Cookery*
- *Salt: A World History* by Mark Kurlansky
- *Scheherazade's Feasts: Food of The Medieval Arab World* by H Salloum, M Salloum & L Salloum
- *In the Beginning there was No Musakka* by Nawal Nasrallah

ABOUT THE AUTHOR

Bethany Kehdy is a Lebanese-American food writer and presenter. Hailed by Yotam Ottolenghi as 'a new champion of Middle Eastern food', her debut cookbook, The Jewelled Kitchen, was selected as one of the notable cookbooks of 2013 by The New York Times. Highlighted by Monocle Magazine as one of four Mediterranean ambassadors, her work on promoting Lebanon as a food destination continues, via her food tour company Taste Lebanon as well as her consultancy work with the Ministry of Tourism. Bethany resides in Lebanon where she also hosts a seasonal-inspired supperclub, called Mawsam.

Published in 2018 by Hardie Grant Books, an imprint of Hardie Grant Publishing

Hardie Grant Books (London)
5th & 6th Floors
52–54 Southwark Street
London SE1 1UN

Hardie Grant Books (Melbourne)
Building 1, 658 Church Street
Richmond, Victoria 3121

hardiegrantbooks.com

British Library Cataloguing-in-Publication Data. A catalogue record for this book is available from the British Library.

The Jewelled Table by Bethany Kehdy
ISBN: 978-1-78488-167-2

Publisher: Kate Pollard
Senior Editor: Molly Ahuja
Publishing Assistant: Eila Purvis
Art Direction: Evi O. Studio | Evi O & Jack Godfrey-Baxter
Photographer: Nassima Rothacker
Photography Assistant: Maria Aversa
Food Stylists: Emily Jonzen and Nicole Herft
Food Stylist Assistant: Rosie Mackean
Prop Stylist: Morag Farquhar
Indexer: Cathy Heath
Colour Reproduction by p2d
Printed and bound in China by Leo Paper Group